"The authors succeeded in wh
intellect. This provocative ye
ante' by leading with my streng
of my team."
—Katy Holt-Larsen, director, Training and Development and Quality Assurance, North American Customer Support, eBay, Inc.

"*Play to Your Strengths* is a rich, easy-to-read conversation about a very
transformative mindset. This book is thorough, thoughtful, and—above
all—practical."
—Phil Sandahl, coauthor, *Co-Active Coaching*

"*Play to Your Strengths* is an excellent resource for anyone who is seeking
to leverage personal strengths more effectively at work and in life. The
poker analogy is very enlightening, even for those of us who don't play
the game! Unlike many assessment exercises, the material in this book is
both entertaining and informative, and very useful as soon as you decide
to apply it. The authors have succeeded in transforming their years of
experience into easily accessible and usable wisdom."
—Dr. Kathy E. Kram, professor of organizational behavior, Boston
University School of Management

"Leavitt and Sigetich deal us a winning hand with *Play to Your
Strengths*! Finally, a breakthrough book that shows leaders how to engage the best talents of each employee to generate amazing results and
achieve competitive advantage. This book, written with clarity, passion, and conviction, assures us that what's needed for success in the
workplace—and in life—is right here inside each of us. A must-read
for leaders everywhere!"
—John Barrasso, M.D., United States Senator

"Stop bluffing. If you're ready for full-flush success, show your pay
hand, buy this book."
—Cliff Hakim, Career Consultant, best-selling author of *Rethinking Work*

"Playing to your strengths is such a simple yet powerful idea, so much
more productive than beating yourself up over shortcomings! And this
book is the 'real deal' for helping you to get clear about your unique
genius and to deploy these special strengths to ensure success."
—Dr. Douglas T. Hall, Morton H. and Charlotte Friedman professor in management, faculty director, MBA Program, Boston University
School of Management

"Within hours of reading just the first few chapters of *Play to Your Strengths* I was able to harness this new perspective, helping me through a challenging situation. It is amazing to be able to look at individuals with the expectation that they can and will be excellent at certain things, and that they will never fully excel at others. It is freeing as an employee and as a manager. Thank you to Leavitt and Sigetich for helping me to see, appreciate, and nurture the glorious potential in my staff members."
—Jamie Lynn Bails, senior vice president, Paradigm Business Solutions, Inc.

"This extraordinary book discusses an aspect of leadership that is often overlooked, misunderstood, and ignored. The single most important realization I've had in my career is that I don't have to, nor can I, do it all. There are those whose skills and insights are superior to mine, and actively endeavoring to get those strengths into the 'game' in a meaningful way is the primary challenge for an effective leader. To do otherwise smothers the very development of others in the up-and-coming leadership progression, which is so critical to the long-lasting success of any organization. I wholeheartedly endorse this book."
—John Inglish, general manager and CEO, Utah Transit Authority

"Every person has talent. The challenge is to recognize it and develop it until it leads. This book offers profound insight into how the unique talents of each person can enrich an organization. A must read...a leap forward in helping all of us discover the great potential within ourselves, in others, and in our organizations."
—Terri Kane, CEO/administrator, Dixie Regional Medical Center

"*Play to Your Strengths* opens doors for leaders to find greater satisfaction and success by applying a new philosophy of professional development to help individuals achieve more of what they really want out of life and to support the very best possible outcomes for their organizations. Now, that's what I call a winning hand for all!"
—Lois Peters Vallerga, FACHE, Former Vice President of Organization Development, St. Charles Medical Centers, Cascade Healthcare Community

"*Play to Your Strengths* is an extremely practical leadership primer. Wonderful and effective stories."
—Oliver K. Myers, Ph.D., Chairman, College of Graduate Business, Utah Campus of the University of Phoenix

PLAY TO YOUR STRENGTHS

STRENGTHS

Stacking the Deck
to Achieve
Spectacular Results
for Yourself and Others

ANDREA SIGETICH AND
CAROL LEAVITT, MBA

**CAREER
PRESS** Career Press, Inc.
Franklin Lakes, N.J.

PLAY TO YOUR STRENGHTS
EDITED BY GINA TALUCCI
TYPESET BY MICHAEL FITZGIBBON
Cover design by Lucia Rossman/Digi Dog Design NYC
Printed in the U.S.A. by Book-mart Press

To order this title, please call toll-free 1-800-CAREER-1 (NJ and Canada: 201-848-0310) to order using VISA or MasterCard, or for further information on books from Career Press.

CAREER
PRESS

The Career Press, Inc., 3 Tice Road, PO Box 687,
Franklin Lakes, NJ 07417
www.careerpress.com

Library of Congress Cataloging-in-Publication Data
Sigetich, Andrea.
    Play to your strengths : stacking the deck to achieve spectacular results for yourself and others / by Andrea Sigetich and Carol Leavitt.
        p. cm.
    Includes bibliographical references and index.
    ISBN-13: 978-1-56414-980-0
    ISBN-10: 1-56414-980-3
    1. Leadership. 2. Management. 3. Success in business. I. Leavitt, Carol. II. Title.

HD57.7.S5225 2007
658.4′09--dc22

                                                                2007041385

Dedication

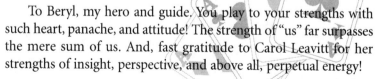

To Beryl, my hero and guide. You play to your strengths with such heart, panache, and attitude! The strength of "us" far surpasses the mere sum of us. And, fast gratitude to Carol Leavitt for her strengths of insight, perspective, and above all, perpetual energy!

—Andrea

To my magnificent parents, Joan and Blaine, whose unconditional love and whole-hearted encouragement have been—and continue to be—instrumental in my discovery of personal strengths. To Mae Taylor, Dorothy Dart, and Andrea Sigetich—my compassionate mentors—and to countless colleagues who have supported me in growing and capitalizing on my strengths throughout a thrilling career. And to Coby Sr., Coby Jr., Ian, and Dave, whose unique and splendid strengths inspire me to amplify my own in this glorious life.

—Carol

Acknowledgments

We are deeply grateful to our clients who, by seeking their own strengths, contributed to this work more than they know.

We appreciate the seminal work of the Gallup organization, which has been highly instrumental in bringing strengths to the forefront.

You have been spared from our incomplete explanations and blunders due to the brilliance of our amazing guest readers! They provided us with insights and perspectives that significantly improved the book. For your time and wisdom, we thank Jamie Bails, LaNae Barber, Donna Billings, Joan Cameron, Steve Camkin, Mary Cary Crawford, Carolyn Esky, Janet Janke, Kathy Kram, Gretchen Rawdon, Teresa Rozic, David Sigetich, and Lois Vallerga.

In addition to our readers, we had others on our support team who bolstered and encouraged us, and also made us get out and play every once in a while! We very much appreciate Jan Baker, Cindy Clemens, Martha Ham, Darci Hansen, Kayla Koeber, Stephanie Martini, Nancy Obymako, Jane Oliver, Mary Ronnow, Charlene Rynders, The Juice Group, and the Wild Women.

Finally, we wish to acknowledge our "silent partner" Beryl Rullman, who read—red pen in hand—every single page of this book in nearly every iteration along the way. We owe you a huge debt of gratitude, and a box of red pens!

Contents

How to Use This Book

We invite you to read, enjoy, and learn from this book using your own strengths. Do you learn best by sitting down and reading an interesting book from cover to cover? Go for it! Do you work best in the seek-and-find method? That works here too! Read the Contents and go directly to a section that intrigues you. Do you want to know the *how* before you care about the *why*? If so, begin by reading the Implementation Ideas section at the end of each chapter. As you begin to travel through this book, do whatever maximizes your strengths! We won't mind; as a matter of fact, we'll love it—and you will enjoy yourself and learn more! Our book is not a mystery, therefore you won't ruin the plot by starting in the middle!

Chapter 1♠: Pat Hand: Playing the Cards You're Dealt, introduces the Strengths Revolution emerging in business, academica, and psychology, because engaging strengths increases personal and organizational success. In it, we define strengths and the innate talents and gifts that underpin skills and passions. Readers explore how strengths are broad and deep, and are so much more than the sum of their experiences, skills, and education. Chapter 1 sets the stage for discovering and applying strengths in your work, your team, your organization, and your life.

In Chapter 2♠: Dealer's Choice: Naming the Game You'll Play, you have the opportunity to name your strengths. You'll create your own leadership brand—the unique differentiator that fuels your leadership success. Often, we do not see our strengths clearly because they are our natural element, the air we breathe. Our strengths are so much a part of us that we cannot imagine anyone *not* doing it the way we do! To find our strengths, we have to pull back, see the strengths that lie within, and become crystal clear about who we are and what we contribute. If you've ever been asked "What is your leadership style?" you'll discover the answer in Chapter 2.

How can you gain clarity about your weaknesses and learn to manage them so they don't steal precious time from playing to your strengths? In Chapter 3♠: Discards: Knowing When to Hold 'em or Fold 'em, you'll identify your weaknesses and—don't despair—create a plan to manage them.

In Chapter 4♠: Showdown: Playing for High Stakes, we explore what to do now that you know your strengths. How does knowing your strengths affect your career, your development, the design of your job, and your personal satisfaction? We consider how you can grow and use your strengths, and align your job to make the most of them.

In Chapter 5♠: Ante Up: Building the Kitty, you'll look at how to invest in your staff's strengths to make everyone richer. As a leader and manager, you already know it is imperative to hire people who will expand your team's effectiveness. You naturally look for skills to augment your staff while boosting its capacity. We explore how strengths improve the basic management processes that you use every day, such as hiring, managing performance, delegating and accountability, and rewarding and developing your people. Having a clear handle on strengths helps you acquire, retain, and inspire truly great talent to achieve your most important goals.

In Chapter 6♠: Ace in the Hole: Uncovering Hidden Strengths, we explore how to mine strengths from the people you lead. We consider how to hold conversations about strengths; how to help others discover their strengths; how to catch them using their strengths; and how to inspire them to build their strengths, creating greater success for the organization. We delve deeply into the most effective tool you have for working with your employees' strengths—the process of coaching. Chapter 6 shows you how to use coaching to engage and motivate others by helping them uncover and use their hidden strengths.

Chapter 7♠: Dolly Parton: Completing the 9-to-5 Straight, highlights strengths in teams of all types—intact, project, temporary, long-term, ad hoc, virtual, or any other. We provide tools you can use to assist in establishing and sustaining a strong team foundation, including chartering, establishing ground rules, creating interlocking accountability, and developing team strengths.

Chapter 8♠: Go All In: Committing the Full House, speaks to senior leaders intrigued by the idea of creating a strengths-based culture. We look at the key people systems and processes found in every organization and show how to shift them to sustain and nurture a culture that redoubles strengths. We believe senior leaders have a huge responsibility and considerable untapped potential to build the most effective organization they can. We also believe strengths-based initiatives provide the key to this goal because using individual strength invariably leads to a stronger organization!

Chapter 9♠: Royal Flush: Winning the Most Important Game, challenges you to further apply your strengths in the most important arena: the game of life. We explore how you can use your strengths in the communities you touch professionally and personally through mentoring, serving your community, and leaving a legacy that surpasses your hopes and expectations.

So let's get cut the deck and get started!

INTRODUCTION

Texas Hold 'Em and the World Series of Poker have grabbed the imagination of the nation. In the business world, application of individual strengths is creating its own storm. As leaders in all walks of life begin to think seriously about strengths, we seek ways to make better use of these—our most important assets. Many who discover their strengths wonder what to do once they have that knowledge. We wrote *Play to Your Strengths* to answer this.

In this, the first comprehensive look at what you can do with your growing knowledge of strengths, we transform strengths and strengths-based work from interesting information to practical application. We write for leaders, managers, and individuals who aspire to discover and apply their strengths fully. Poker is a great metaphor because, no matter what hand you're dealt, you always have the opportunity to play it to your advantage.

In life, we each hold a perfect hand: our unique array of strengths. Focusing on strengths builds our productivity and that of the communities in which we live, work, and play. Our wish for you is deep and clear knowledge of your own strengths, and we hope to inspire you to share this imperative knowledge with others, building the capacity and the contribution of every individual and every organization.

Throughout these pages, we sometimes write about our experience learning to apply our own strengths and working with the strengths of our leadership clients. When we refer to "Andrea" or "Carol" – that's us!

We chose to address the gender-pronoun issue of him/her through a relatively non-traditional approach. In the odd-numbered chapters, the generic individual is a "he." In even-numbered chapters, it's "she." Of course, we include and honor leaders of both genders!

—Andrea and Carol

A POKER PRIMER

Poker is a card game of skill with many forms and variations. Despite the many different types, some basics apply to most poker games; the hand ranking is one such basic. The ranking of hands (without wild cards) is:

1. Royal Flush: AKQJ10 of the same suit (A♠, K♠, Q♠, J♠, 10♠).

2. Straight Flush: Five consecutively ranked cards of the same suit (4♦, 5♦, 6♦, 7♦, 8♦).

3. Four of a Kind: Four cards of the same rank (2♥, 2♠, 2♦, 2♣, X).

4. Full House: Three cards of one rank and two of another (3♣, 3♥, 3♠, 10♦, 10♥). This full house is expressed as "Threes over 10s."

5. Flush: Any five cards of the same suit (3♣, 7♣, 9♣, 10♣, K♣).

6. Straight: Five consecutively ranked cards of more than one suit (2♦, 3♠, 4♥, 5♣, 6♦).

7. Three of a Kind: Three cards of the same rank (K♣, K♠, K♦, X, X).

8. Two pair: Two cards of one rank and two cards of another rank (3♣, 3♥, J♦, J♠, *X*).

9. One pair: Two cards of the same rank (9♠, 9♣, *X, X, X*)

10. High Card (K♣, *X, X, X, X*).

CHAPTER ONE
PAT HAND:
PLAYING THE CARDS
YOU'RE DEALT

Pat Hand: Holding or being dealt a complete hand.[1]

In an obscure old spaghetti western, a poker game (Five-Card Draw), is under way. Outside, dust and tumbleweeds blow by. Inside, tough, determined cowboys and outlaws are playing for far more than the money in the pot: they're vying for bragging rights. Five cards are dealt facedown to each player, and each player, in turn, requests replacement cards. Except Luke. Maintaining a straight, unflinching poker face, Luke is satisfied with his hand. He calls every bet. One at a time, certain of holding the winning hand, each player flips over his cards. Luke, the last player to reveal, slowly turns over his cards to expose the winning hand—a full house, kings over 10s. He gathers the pile of money from the table and walks away triumphant, ever the hero.

Similar to Luke in this old movie, each of us already holds a pat hand. Your pat hand—your complete hand—is your own unique combination of strengths. You may hold four eights, while my pat hand is a full house, and our colleague holds a flush. Each hand is different, and each hand is sound. It's perfect as it is; you need no other cards. Play to your strengths and you'll walk away triumphant, ever the hero.

Exploiting Strengths

Now replaced by spectacular Wild West mega-movies, the old westerns have come a long way. So, too, has leadership. In the old, dusty days of leadership thinking, an aspiring leader would:

- ♠ decide what competencies a good leader should possess.
- ♠ compare his weaknesses to those competencies.
- ♠ fix the gap between his weakness and the competency.
- ♠ remember his strengths.

By contrast, in our enlightened contemporary times, the new *Play-to-Your-Strengths* way to build leadership is to:

- ♠ decide what competencies a good leader should possess.
- ♠ compare your strengths to those competencies.
- ♠ develop opportunities to use your strengths more.
- ♠ manage your weaknesses.

It is our strengths that offer us our deepest satisfaction and sustainable successes. Our strengths drive our skills, knowledge, and behaviors. You may succeed as a leader because of your inherent talent for orchestrating action, and your colleague may succeed as a leader because of his gift for building relationships. It is vital that we understand our foundational strengths so we can choreograph our lives to manifest and actualize our strengths.

We define strengths as the innate talents and gifts that underpin skills and passions. The strengths are the base, and the skills are built on top of them. When we operate from our true strengths, our work is easy—and magnificent!

When you claim your strengths and teach your followers to do likewise, you'll do more than just put those strengths to use; you'll discover additional gifts, passions, knowledge, talents, and skills. Engaging personal strengths and the strengths of others is how successful leaders emerge. Maximizing strengths is how these same leaders reach the pinnacle of their careers.

Even though a few people excel through massive efforts to overcome weaknesses, the majority of us find that the pathway to success lies in leveraging our strengths. Typically, we only achieve mediocre or adequate performance in an area of true weakness, even with the best training.

> ♠
>
> *It takes far more energy to improve from imcompetence to mediocrity than to improve from first-rate performance to excellence.*
> *—Peter Drucker*
>
> ♠

Do you really want to spend your precious resources of time, money, and energy trying to fix your weaknesses, and achieve only mediocrity? Do you want to spend your department's or organization's entire training budget striving for mediocre performance? We sincerely hope not. Unfortunately, many leaders and organizations still try to develop talent through the old paradigm of fixing weaknesses. Now, there's a better way. *Play to Your Strengths* turns this old, inefficient, misguided paradigm topsy-turvy.

The Tough Truth

We experience our greatest joys and successes when we use our strengths in our work, and in the rest of our lives, too. It's a no-brainer, really. To some extent, you've already designed your life to play to your innate strengths, through the courses you selected in school, the jobs you took, and the career you chose. It seems the natural, intuitive way to make these decisions.

Yet, research conducted by the Gallup Organization, surveying literally millions of employees, reveals that less than one in five employees uses his strengths at work every day.[2] That's less than 20 percent! It's a sad testimony, isn't it? What is the other 80 percent doing? Are they using their strengths once in a while? Occasionally? Not at all? Do they even know what their strengths are?

Are you one of the five people who plays to her strengths every day? What about the people you lead? Are only 20 percent of them bringing their strengths to work? There is a huge up-side opportunity for leaders and organizations to increase this number to 30, 50, or even 100 percent!

Our strengths "have a yearning quality to them."[3] They want to be used. We feel good, we feel strong, we are good when we use our strengths. We are sustained, renewed, invigorated, and fulfilled. Time flies when we're in the flow of using our strengths. We contribute the best of who we are when we're challenged and inspired to use our strengths. How can we justify 80 percent of our employees *not* having this experience every day? How can we rationalize this waste of human resources? How can we tolerate neglecting our own performance potential and ultimate job—and life—fulfillment?

The Myth of Well-Roundedness

Once upon a time, the animals came together and founded a school with six subjects: swimming, crawling, running, jumping, climbing, and flying. At first the duck was the best swimmer, but she wore out the webs of her feet in running class, and then couldn't swim as well. The dog was the best runner, but he crashed in flying class and injured a leg. The rabbit started out as the best jumper, but he fell in climbing class and hurt his back. At the end of the school year, the class valedictorian was the eel, who could do a little bit of everything, but nothing very well.

In our society, we learn that being well-rounded is the path to success. In school we read, write, add, subtract, create scientific experiments, shoot baskets, and perhaps play a ukulele, on a quest to expand our skills and knowledge. In childhood, this is an important developmental task. We expose children to many opportunities so they can explore their inherent talents, interests, and strengths. As we grow older we narrow our focus. We declare a major in college. We apply for specific jobs with specific characteristics. By our 20s, we find ourselves faced with a decision concerning the imperative question: Will I be a carpenter, a software developer, or a veterinarian?

Some who follow the path of strengths naturally expand into management and leadership roles. When we leave our role as successful individual contributors and enter management, once again, the pesky "myth of well-roundedness" comes into play. Suddenly we must *also* be good at managing people, allocating resources, creating a big picture, and setting a strategic direction while simultaneously designing and implementing specific tactics to accomplish that vision. We learn to manage budgets, work effectively with customers and clients, create solutions, influence up and across the organization, market our team products and services, track expenditures, lead teams, lead individuals, negotiate…you get the idea! Eventually we ask: "Can I possibly have *all* of these skills as my strengths?" Not likely!

We find true success when we clearly identify our strengths and leverage them. One of Andrea's long-time executive coaching clients is John Inglish, general manager and CEO of the Utah Transit Authority. John is a well-known and highly respected player in his profession. His picture often appears on the cover of transit journals, and he excels at creating a vision of what is possible. Through his ability to see and communicate that vision, he engages others in his quest—in Utah, across the nation, and throughout the world. He lights a fire under his staff, his board, his industry, and his customers. He is a leader, naturally and appropriately positioned at the top of his organization.

But John doesn't implement. He is bored if he has to design the steps to create his vision. He knows it's not his strength, and he hires others for their strengths as implementers—the "doers" who put substance around his vision. Without people who excel at making things happen, his vision will not come to fruition. He knows, beyond a shadow of a doubt, that he'll waste his time, and the organization's money, if he tries to become a doer; it's simply not his strength. His insightful and clear awareness of his weakness, and the actions he takes to compensate for it, free his time, passion, and energy to communicate his organization's vision to those who can affect it—stakeholders, legislators, customers, staff, and funding sources.

John is an outstanding example of a leader who truly plays to his strengths because he knows and articulates them. He creates opportunities to use his strong pat hand to forward his vision. What he sees is reliable and enjoyable transportation that makes the best use of technology, interfaces seamlessly with the population, and is environmentally responsible. All who are touched by his legacy benefit from his awareness of his strengths. He is not well-rounded, but his team is! It is this combined team strength that allows him to effectively apply his strengths, and only his strengths, to the cutting-edge opportunities he creates.

If strengths are a source of great success, accomplishment, and fulfillment, what could be better than doing a job in which we excel? Nothing...except doing it all the time! Our strengths move us toward excellence and bring us an emotional benefit: deep and lasting joy.

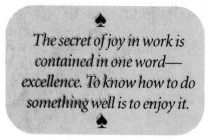

The secret of joy in work is contained in one word—excellence. To know how to do something well is to enjoy it.

Playing to our strengths also builds self-confidence, self-esteem, and honest self-assessment. Know and use what you do well and you'll taste real fulfillment. Apply your strengths broadly and you'll do work you love. Leverage your strengths and you will be more successful. Contribute your strengths to the organization and you will lead with ease and power.

One of Andrea's strengths is recognizing potential in others and knowing clearly how to challenge them to maximize their potential. In her first job at GE, she had a mentor, Chuck Phillips, who taught her to recognize and exploit her strengths so others could benefit. She refined her strengths and used them to develop others in her first management job. Then, she expanded her strengths by deepening her knowledge in adult development. She consciously created a road map to get *better* at using her strengths. Not only did she achieve personal and organizational success, but she also had lots of fun becoming a leader!

Imagine training Fred Astaire to become an engineer, making him "well-rounded," while ignoring his legendary strength in dance. Who, then, would dance with Ginger?! The message is clear: recognize, develop, and play to your strengths—*not* to your weaknesses. When you do play to your strengths, you may not be well-rounded, but you will be extraordinarily successful.

The Strengths Revolution

The work of the Gallup Organization—and the leadership of authors Marcus Buckingham, Donald O. Clifton, Tom Rath, Martin Seligman, and others—has accomplished a monumental task: to spark a "Strengths Revolution." Based on our own work with hundreds of leaders in Fortune-500 organizations, nonprofits, and entrepreneurial start-up companies throughout the last few years, we are thrilled to help lead the revolution by encouraging you to bring strengths to your leadership. The time is right for us to acknowledge that, similar to Luke in the old spaghetti western, everyone already has a pat hand—their perfect and unique array of strengths.

In *Play to Your Strengths*, we will show you how to gain a solid understanding of your strengths and your weaknesses. We offer you a strategy for addressing your weaknesses once and for all, while

A person can perform only from strength. One cannot build performance on weaknesses, let alone on something one cannot do at all.
—Peter Drucker

freeing up energy to develop your strengths. We explore how to guide the people you lead to identify and use their strengths, how to build a team that plays to its strengths, and how to design an entire strengths-based organization that supports and sustains these engaging efforts. The strengths movement is growing as more and more leaders recognize the power of focusing on strengths. We invite you to join the revolution!

Dr. Jim Harter of the Gallup Organization and Dr. Frank Schmidt of the University of Iowa, asked 12 questions of 198,000 employees in 7,989 teams in 36 organizations, including, "Do you know what is expected of you at work?" and, "Do you feel your opinion counts?" They sought to discover which employee attitudes and opinions differentiated high-performing teams from low-performing teams, so they also collected data on team and business performance—productivity, profitability, customer satisfaction, employee turnover, and safety.

The question with the strongest correlation to business outcomes was, "At work, do you have the opportunity to do what you do best every day?" Teams of employees who said they played to their strengths outperformed teams who said they did not—even when the work was identical.[4]

Engagement is a popular concept and tool in organizations these days, because engagement is the most important measure of employee productivity. Organizations small and large are seeking ways to engage workers, often using surveys to measure engagement. One item rated on most of these surveys—"having the opportunity to use my strengths every day at work"—is *highly* correlates with employee engagement. Recent research findings by Krueger and Killham in the *Gallup Management Journal* strongly suggest that when companies emphasize strengths development, both innovation and creativity increase. Further, the research reveals "a significant relationship among worker engagement, manager focus on strengths, and creativity between colleagues." Workers become more engaged when their manager focuses on strengths and strength development. They are also much more likely to share ideas with colleagues at work, essential to improving innovation in organizations.

Businesses have long known the value of identifying and maximizing the organization's strengths, commonly called "core competencies." Remember when Jack Welch took over General Electric in the early 1980s and told each division they must be number-1 or number-2 in their market or he would shut them down? GE narrowed its focus to its enormously successful core competencies. Other successful organizations develop their core competencies—their strengths—by refining and improving core products and outsourcing the rest. For a long time we've known we need to develop and market our strong points—rather than waste effort on the things we perform with mere mediocrity. This works for organizations and, not surprisingly, it works for individuals, too.

Many organizations (Wells Fargo, Ann Taylor, Intel, FedEx, Best Buy, and Accenture, to name a few) are implementing strengths-based initiatives. All new managers at Toyota attend a three-day "Great Manager training program" to learn how to identify the strengths of their employees. New managers at Yahoo take an online survey to pinpoint their strengths. If you're a soccer coach, Major League Soccer will gladly sign you up for its strengths-based coaching course where they teach you to hand out "green cards" to your young athletes, drawing attention to a particularly good pass or tackle, rather than the traditional punitive yellow and red cards that point out what the child didn't do well.[5]

27

In their book *Positive Organizational Scholarship*, in the chapter "Investing in Strengths," Donald Clifton and James Harter summarize the research on strengths-based organizations in this way: "Workplaces with a higher proportion of employees indicating they 'have the opportunity to do what they do best every day' are more productive, have higher customer loyalty, and have lower turnover. Businesses studied that adopted a strengths-based approach to individual development have seen the greatest gains in employee engagement, and hence productivity."

While strengths awareness is growing in business, there is a simultaneous strengths revolution occurring in psychology, known as "positive psychology." Traditionally, psychology embraced a disease model of human nature, with a strong emphasis on what needs to be healed in the client. "Positive psychology proposes that it is time to correct this imbalance and to challenge the assumptions of the disease model. Positive psychology calls for as much focus on strength as on weakness, as much interest in building the best things in life as in repairing the worst, as much attention to fulfilling the lives of healthy people as healing the wounds of the distressed."[6]

Universities, where great thinking (often) takes place, are leading the way. At the University of Michigan Business School, faculty researchers are pioneering business processes that build upon each person's unique talents and capabilities rather than trying to fix performance shortfalls. Students engage in a process called the "Reflective Best Self Exercise" in which each discovers his or her own "best self" and determine ways to contribute value to others. The faculty goal is to enable students to become "active architects" of their jobs, developing and using their talents and building relationships with others.[7]

Notables such as Martin Seligman, Ph.D.—often called the "Father of Positive Psychology," and past president of the American Psychological Association—as well as Mihaly Csikszentmihalyi, Ph.D., Christopher Peterson, Ph.D., and others have learned a great deal about strengths through recent research. Identifying and applying strengths leads to satisfaction, productivity, fulfillment, and, yes, that elusive commodity—happiness. The character strengths of gratitude, hope, zest, curiosity, and love are "robustly associated" with life and work satisfaction. The strength of zest—enthusiasm and energy—is particularly associated with high engagement among workers who regard their work as a calling, instead of simply a way to make money.[8]

If we want to engage our workforce (a really great idea whose time has come) let's offer them opportunities to play to their strengths every day!

Strengths—The Payoff for Individuals

When we focus on identifying, using, and developing our strengths, we become even more competent at what we do well, which produces a formidable set of benefits. When working from your strong hand, you:

- ♠ create great results.
- ♠ gain self-awareness, self-esteem, and self-confidence.
- ♠ become more engaged.
- ♠ have greater clarity and confidence about career and life decisions.
- ♠ naturally find a deeper sense of fulfillment.
- ♠ become inspired to grow and learn; you approach development with eagerness.
- ♠ know what to say no to and what to say yes to.
- ♠ have more fun, which inspires you to gain even more success!
- ♠ increase your energy because strengths are self-renewing.
- ♠ lower your defensiveness about your weaknesses; they simply become less important.

Strengths—The Payoff for Organizations

It's not only individuals who benefit. The organization realizes these advantages:

- ♠ We improve employee productivity, engagement, and retention when we focus on strengths.

- ♠ We increase customer loyalty.

- ♠ We raise the percentage of workers who say they "have the opportunity to use my strengths at work every day."

- ♠ Development opportunities engage the hearts and minds of employees.

- ♠ New learning sticks are necessary because employees are engaged in something they care about.

- ♠ Partnerships and alliances, inside and outside the organization, are more powerful because everyone does what they do best.

- ♠ Succession management and development planning are on-target and not-wasted efforts, because we don't squander resources on low-return, deficit-based training.

- ♠ We create clearer, more compelling career paths for employees.

- ♠ Coaching and mentoring are more effective and have a stronger affect on the recipients.

- ♠ Managers provide clearer performance feedback.

What About Weakness?

We know some of you may be thinking, "But I have weaknesses. I can't simply ignore them," and you're right. As much as we wish it were so, weaknesses do not just fall off the radar screen because we want them to. Sometimes (though not as often as we might think) a

30

weakness can be a career derailer, and we must improve from poor to adequate performance in that area to continue in a particular job or career. While strengths are inherent, innate gifts, weaknesses at work are often simple gaps in skill or bit of knowledge. The vast majority of the time, we need only to add a missing skill or knowledge to our repertoire. To learn this new skill easily and effectively, we determine which of our *strengths* will assist us.

We can also *choose* to work on a weakness or a skill gap for fun, interest, or intrigue. We may simply *want* to speak French or play lacrosse even though it doesn't maximize our strengths, but so what? We do it because we choose to! Unfortunately, many people enrolled in training courses and seminars at work are *sent* to the class to correct a weakness. All too often the expensive class, self-help book, or time with a coach—designed to "correct" a weakness—serves only to frustrate the participant even more, so they learn *just* enough to get by.

That limited success often has a short shelf life because, if it is a weakness and we are not inspired by it, we likely won't sustain it through practice.

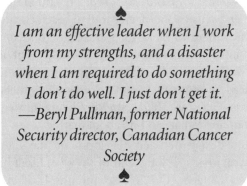

♠
I am an effective leader when I work from my strengths, and a disaster when I am required to do something I don't do well. I just don't get it.
—Beryl Pullman, former National Security director, Canadian Cancer Society
♠

We all have a weakness or two that may never be corrected. Are we suggesting that you simply ignore them? Well, yes and no. We propose that you learn about your weaknesses and put a plan in place to manage them. Then you'll be able to concentrate on using your strengths, allowing your weaknesses to become negligible.

We used to work in the "weakness" arena (we moan, "mea culpa!"). Now, older and wiser, we know that weakness development has serious limitations. Individual reliance on strengths produces incredible personal and organizational success. Manage, mitigate, and reduce a weakness when you must—when it is getting in the way of fully applying your strengths—but otherwise, play the hand you're dealt—build and expand your strengths.

Weakness: The Curse of Development Plans

A 360-degree feedback process (soliciting insight from peers, direct reports, and the boss) is a popular organizational tool for developing leaders. While it provides helpful data on what the leader does well and what needs improvement, the 360-degree focuses on *competencies*—behaviors and skills—*not* on inherent gifts and strengths. When we use a 360-degree tool to coach clients, it's difficult to convince them to look (for more than 10 seconds) at the *positive* capabilities others see in them. Instead, client after client zeroes in on weaknesses. Like a compass spinning around to point north, these leaders desperately want to know what others think are their weaknesses. They ask, "How am I not living up to what I and others expect of me? What can I do about that?"

They often design detailed development plans, targeted at overcoming weaknesses: "By the end of the year, I will be a highly effective budget manager." Or, "In three months, I will excel at time management." But three months never comes, much less a year! Similar to New Year's resolutions, the gild falls off the lily in six or eight weeks because working on a weakness can be draining and not much fun. With their plates overflowing with work priorities, challenging management issues, rising performance expectations, and problems to resolve, these leaders and managers may find it hard to become inspired or motivated to overcome weaknesses. And frankly, in most situations, the payoff is minor. If adequate performance is as good as it gets, is it worth allocating limited resources to develop a leader's weaknesses?

Powerful, effective leadership development requires the right tools and processes, along with the right mindset. We must focus on *strengths*, first by identifying them and then applying them to address those weaknesses that must be corrected. We will have much greater leverage when we bolster our strengths, so they can compensate for and manage our weaknesses.

The Heretics Speak

♠

...we all have our own unique set of strengths, weaknesses, and past experiences, which means we can bring something to the table that nobody else in the world possibly could.
—Miles Levin, an 18-year-old with terminal cancer

♠

We know this may be heretical to some, but we believe leaders secretly *yearn* to know their strengths.

They want to discover and shout from the rooftop, "I am *great* at this! Bring it on!" When leaders find their strengths and create plans for expanding them, the sky is the limit! These leaders begin to ask:

33

"If communicating with large groups is a strength of mine, how can I do it more? Can I change my job and do more of what I excel at and love? Can I present at trade conferences, to customers, or to employees in other divisions or locations? Can I teach what I know? Who is the up-and-coming presenter in my organization? Does he need a mentor? How much more will I contribute to the organization if I fully utilize my strengths? How can I underscore this strength to achieve higher levels of success?" Identifying our individual strengths is a win-win for the individual *and* the organization! You can't beat that!

We can churn out a decent budget when we have to, or lead a project if we must, but these roles are tiring if they do not play to our strengths. We leave work exhausted, our energy consumed. Our work is much more powerful and effective when built on a foundation of strength. When we work from our strong suit, our energy is high. We are thrilled, motivated, excited, and *compelled* to do more!

Marcus Buckingham and Donald O. Clifton, in their book, *Now, Discover Your Strengths* (The Free Press, 2001), define strength as "consistent near-perfect performance in an activity." That's a high bar, but when you really think about it, isn't it true? Consistent near-perfect performance! When I am *that* good, how can I *not* shine? How can I *not* contribute my talents to the world?

Buckingham and Clifton also assert that most organizations have two flawed assumptions about the people who work with them: first, that every human being can be competent in almost anything; and, second, that our greatest room for growth is in the area of our greatest weakness. In truth, knowing our weaknesses will help us prevent failure, but not achieve excellence; we achieve excellence when we build on our strengths. Most organizations hire for skill and experience, and take for granted an employee's strengths.

When the honeymoon is over and we notice blemishes and deficiencies, we attempt to close the skills gap and "fix" the weaknesses. We do damage control, not development. We waste our precious resources on training to a weakness, and neither we nor the organization have much to show for it. Imagine what might happen if we hired for strengths and then encouraged each person to use them to his full capacity. How successful would our organizations be? How successful would *we* be?

♠

Once
Looking at the same flowering weeds
Trembling in the breeze
I sensed their weakness.
Today
Seeing the same weeds
Trembling in the breeze
I realize their strength.
—Tomihiro Hoshimo,
"Journey to the Wind"

♠

In their book *Soar With Your Strengths*, Donald Clifton and Paula Nelson discuss a three-year study conducted by the University of Nebraska to determine the most effective techniques for teaching speed-reading. The results of this study are interesting and revealing. The *poor* readers in the study began with an average reading speed of 90 words per minute. As a result of the techniques, these students increased their reading speed and comprehension to 150 words per minute—a 67-percent improvement. The *excellent* readers, who entered the study reading 350 words per minute, raised their reading speed and comprehension to 2,900 words per minutes—an 800 percent improvement! Dramatic results can be achieved from building on strengths!

The Sea and the Desert

Strength-based development is a new topic, and yet seems as old as the sea. Plato said, "Nothing can be more absurd than the practice that prevails in our country of men and women not following pursuits with all their strengths." The concept of strengths has been around a long time.

And there is much work yet to do. We look forward to academicians and practitioners studying the affect of strengths on individual and organizational success. Because we are in the embryonic stage of the new Strengths Revolution, we need a better strengths lexicon and better tools to help people clearly and easily identify their strengths. Our society has created a giant industry built around fixing weaknesses. However, we already see training and development providers thinking about strengths and developing strengths-related tools for organizations. We believe this trend will continue to build—because it works.

When talking about the Strengths Revolution on *The Today Show*, Marcus Buckingham said, "If you want a movement, you need zealots."[9] While we never considered ourselves zealots for anything (well, maybe the red rock area of southern Utah!), we're ready and willing to take a stand as zealots for strengths. We know the power of strengths—personally, professionally, and viscerally. We know not only for ourselves, but we also know from the hundreds of leaders we've coached and the organizations signing on to the Strengths Revolution.

If you want to make your dreams come true, wake up. Wake up to your own strength. Wake up to the role you play in your own destiny. Wake up to the power you have to choose what you think, do, and say.
—*Keith Ellis*

We know that using strengths builds self-confidence and enables us to become strong and authentic leaders. To play to your strengths is the greatest contribution you can make to your organization and your career.

For our part, we will continue to encourage leaders to implement strengths discovery and strengths-based development. We urge you to do the same. You already hold a pat hand. Get in the game to play and win!

Pat Hand

You've read about the Strengths Revolution and the cutting-edge actions that organizations and individuals are taking to play to their strengths. You've gained a sense of why this work is so very important. In Chapter 2♠, we'll show you how to assess and articulate your strengths, so you, too, can play your pat hand—your own perfect and unique array of strengths.

Implementation Ideas

PONDER YOUR STRENGTHS

Start wondering about, noticing, and considering your strengths. In the chapters ahead, we introduce a process to discover your strengths; however, you might enjoy beginning your discovery process now! Begin to notice when you are naturally creative, when you are intensely engaged and invigorated, and when you feel confident and strong.

GAIN SOME WISDOM FROM ANOTHER PROFESSION

If the field of positive psychology interests you, there are some intriguing resources to consult. A great Website is *www.authentichappiness.com.* You may find it interesting to read a book by Mihaly Csikszentmihalyi on the concept of "flow," such as *Good Business: Leadership, Flow, and the Making of Meaning* (Penguin, 2004). (Here's how you pronounce his name, in case you want to ask for one of his books at the bookstore. It's "cheeks-sent-me-high." Helps, doesn't it?)

Our particular favorite in this field is a textbook—one that keeps your interest and even makes you laugh once in a while, *A Primer in Positive Psychology* by Christopher Peterson (Oxford University Press, 2006).

BE INSPIRED!

We thought you might like to reread Nelson Mandela's words, in his 1994 inaugural speech, quoting Marianne Williamson:

Our deepest fear is not that we are inadequate. Our deepest fear is that we are powerful beyond measure. It is our light, not our darkness that most frightens us. We ask ourselves, 'Who am I to be brilliant, gorgeous, talented, and fabulous?' Actually, who are you not to be? You are a child of God; your playing small doesn't serve the world.

Catch a Flick

"Spaghetti western" is a nickname for a broad sub-genre of films that emerged in the mid-1960s, most often produced by Italian studios. Some of the best-known spaghetti westerns are the *Man With No Name* trilogy (starring Clint Eastwood), *A Fistful of Dollars* (1964), and *The Good, the Bad and the Ugly* (1966). Many of the films were shot in the Spanish desert of Almería, which greatly resembles the landscape of the American Southwest.

The term "spaghetti western" was originally used disparagingly, but by the 1980s many of these low-budget Italian minimalist films came to be held in high regard, particularly because of the influence they had in redefining the entire area of a western. Rent one and watch Clint use his copious strengths to become a superstar! (Source: *www.wikipedia.org*)

A

CHAPTER TWO
DEALER'S CHOICE:
NAMING THE GAME
YOU'LL PLAY

Dealer's Choice: In home games, a rule that permits the dealer to name which poker game is to be played that hand.

Winning the Olympic gold medal in ping-pong is a Chinese tradition. At the 1984 Olympics, a curious reporter asked the coach of the Chinese team about the training regimen that produces such consistently excellent results. The coach replied, "We practice eight hours per day perfecting our strengths. If you develop your strengths to the maximum, the strength becomes so great it overwhelms the weakness. Our winning player, you see, plays only his forehand. Even though he cannot play backhand and his competition knows he cannot play backhand, his forehand is so invincible that it cannot be beaten."[1]

What a surprise! The best player on the best ping-pong team in the world couldn't play backhand! He plays to his strength so well that he overcomes his weakness.

We practice eight hours per day perfecting our strengths. If you develop your strengths to the maximum, the strength became so great it overwhelms the weakness.
—coach of the Olympic gold medal Chinese Ping Pong Team

His forehand is that strong—and he continues to develop his skill by growing and perfecting his strength.

What is your forehand? What do you do so well now that doing it even better will overwhelm your weaknesses? We—all of us—truly do excel at our strengths. You're the dealer in this game of life. You get to name the game you play; you might as well play to your strength. Our core strengths are like a software program running all the time—formatting, saving edits, controlling the parameters, the style, and the design. Our core strengths provide a similar framework; they run behind the scene and below our radar screen. And similar to the master template that opens when we need a new document, they, too, create options for us and design how we see the world.

We often don't see our strengths clearly because they are the sea in which we swim. Does a fish see the water? Do the birds see the air? Our strengths are the context in which we live and breathe and work and play. Our colleague Abigail Morgan remarked, "Strengths are like our skin. They surround us and encompass us. And, we need a mirror in order to see them all!"

When it comes to strengths, we may not have the objectivity or the perspective to identify our strengths on our own. What impresses others can seem mundane and ordinary to us. Discovering your unique strengths requires standing outside yourself and suspending for one moment the way you see the world. The way you see your world probably *is* your strength, but because you see it through your own eyes you don't recognize it.

Let's assume one of your strengths is applying learning from past actions, successes, and failures. With this strength, you put issues into perspective based on understanding the past and the context in which the issue was created. So, if an issue is perplexing, you look backward to your experience and history and search for a pattern or a story that sheds light on the current situation. This is simply the way your mind works.

Now imagine that your colleague's strength is seeing the big picture. She naturally and easily sees linkages among seemingly disparate pieces of information. By the way, Buckingham and Clifton call this linking of disparate ideas "Ideation" in their strengths assessment, the Clifton StrengthsFinder (more on how you can take the Clifton StrengthsFinder later in Implementation Ideas). Your colleague clearly possesses Ideation as a strength.

How differently will you and your colleague see the issue at hand? Your perspectives are likely to diverge, to contrast significantly. You see the issue in light of history, in the context surrounding it—recalling prior events. Your colleague sees the current big picture. She may not see the history at all, but will see how this issue links to other situations occurring in the organization right now. These different perspectives can be a source of argument, frustration, or disagreement as the two of you attempt to communicate. If you can be objective, you'll discover that these differences lead you to a broader and clearer understanding of the issue at hand. When you both contribute your strengths to the issue, you'll arrive at a richer, more varied, more powerful, and more complete perspective.

If you have traveled a path in life that feels like a mistake or a false start, you probably wish someone had told you your strengths much earlier in life. If someone told you what you would do so well, what you'd excel in, what you'd love doing beyond all other things, wouldn't that be a gift of immeasurable proportions?

Your 21ST Birthday

Turning 21 is a rite of passage into adulthood. It's a birthday we anticipate for years. Perhaps you experienced trepidation ("Oh my gosh, now I have to be responsible!"). Perhaps you felt elation ("Finally, I've reached adulthood!"). Maybe you had a big celebration, replete with alcohol. Maybe it passed quietly, with only a close friend or two. Whatever the day held for you, roll back the video to your 21st birthday, and add a scene....

Imagine you walk into a bright, sunny kitchen early on the morning of your 21st birthday. You grab your favorite beverage and see, in the center of the kitchen table, a small box, elegantly wrapped in shiny paper and tied securely with a velvet bow. You haven't a clue who left this box for you, but it certainly is intriguing! You pull one end of the bow and it comes undone. Under the paper is a small, handmade, inlaid wooden box. You take a deep breath and gently pry open the lid. What's inside?

You probably know what it is—yes, it's your strengths. Five of your most powerful core strengths in all their shining glory. There's a sparkling diamond; a deep, intense, blue sapphire; a gorgeous green emerald; a glimmering fire opal; and a ruby, brilliant red. The gems are there for you to take and use as you choose. This is a profound gift, a surprising gift—and yet, there's something very familiar about these gemstones. You know these strengths intimately, precisely, and acutely. A perfect gift!

God gives each of us special talents and gifts. It is both our priviledge and our duty to make the most of them.
—Robert E. Allen

Imagine if each of us received this gift as we crossed the threshold into adulthood—clear and perfect knowledge of our specific and unique strengths—a diamond, a sapphire, an emerald, an opal, and a ruby.

Five strengths to make our perfect poker hand! With this acute knowledge and insight about our strengths, we could clearly see our options to choose. We would know what career to pursue; what activities will bring us happiness and fulfillment; and how to create and design the successes we want in our lives. These strengths shine their lights on how we might choose to live our lives. Yeow! This is magnificent!

But I'm 41, not 21.

Unfortunately, not many of us have our strengths presented to us in a box on our 21st birthday. We have to explore and ponder to find our strengths. As illustrated in the following graphic on page 46, there are a number of different sources—internal and external—to help reveal our strengths. We need to rely on inputs from others. We have to fight years of misguided conditioning that keeps us focused on our weaknesses and what we allegedly need to improve, and we need to look deep inside to find the underlying talent—the deep strength—that has, throughout the years, manifested itself in specific tasks.

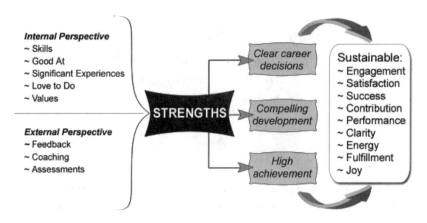

If I'm good at playing the piano, for example, I might answer a question about my strengths by saying, "I excel at concertos. I do a great interpretation of Brandenburg." I have specialized, focused, refined, and improved my skills so much that I no longer see that the underlying strengths I have are a marvelous ear for tone as well as a love for music. If my real strengths are my ear and my love, and not concertos, then I can expand the scope of my work and my contribution in an amazing array of activities. I can teach young children to play in a band. I could become a buyer for a music store. I can start playing rock and roll—or try a different instrument. I can apply my strengths to my current work and rebuild my enthusiasm and passion. I can learn more about the history of concertos for my own edification or to offer a workshop to other enthusiasts.

Because we are good at something does not necessarily mean it's a strength. The strength needs to be fed by passion. We have a colleague who excels at administrative tasks, but hates them. Her strengths are creativity and design. She's not happy and fulfilled in her work as an administrator because she hasn't combined her talents with her passions.

Our friend Richard is an astronomer; he has passion for the skies and powerful strengths in analysis, creating models, and learning. He is a genius, combining his passion and his talents. Now in retirement, he teaches adults about astronomy, and he studies and explores the history of astronomy. He and his wife also paint historic scenes from astronomy that he uses in his classes and to illustrate his books. He continues to tap into his deep passion and scientific strengths.

It's interesting to see how Richard builds his strengths and passions, and how the piano player does likewise, through broader application of a deep strength. It's similar for those of us who work in organizations. In many cases, as we climbed the career ladder, we became generalists, due to the myth of well-roundedness. That's when we lost sight of our underlying, deeper strengths. How do we become really clear about our strengths? Let's meet Michael, an amalgamation of our best clients, whose story continues throughout this book and guides us on our journey of understanding and applying strengths.

Michael

Michael is director of sales for the western region at B2B Printers. During his performance review last week, Michael's boss Jane told him that she was "a little disappointed." While Michael is a solid performer, he has lost a bit of the enthusiasm and spark he once had, and now seems to be "scattered." He is having trouble delegating, and holds on to too many sales activities. Jane knows Michael has excellent leadership skills, but she doesn't see him applying those skills as often as he could. Because Jane believes in him and feels Michael has more to contribute, she thought it would be useful for the two of them to unearth Michael's strengths, and to focus his efforts where he excels.

When Jane asked about his strengths, Michael said he was good at inspiring people to do better work, at following up on leads, at closing sales, and at selling his ideas to upper management. Jane agreed. She asked Michael to complete the Clifton StrengthsFinder assessment to help him clarify his underlying strengths. They discussed how to notice clues to recognizing these natural innate talents and strengths. Here are some of their ideas:

♠   We feel a pull toward activities that naturally make good use of our strengths. If adventure is one of our strengths, we're naturally drawn toward adventurous opportunities. Our strengths call to us.

♠   We may enter the state of "flow" when we're working from our strengths and become so engrossed in an activity, we lose track of time.

♠   We experience high satisfaction when we complete challenges that make good use of our strengths. More importantly, we experience high energy when using our strengths. Using our weaknesses depletes us; using our strengths energizes us. When we notice the situations and activities that invigorate us, we begin to see our strengths in action.

♠   Learning is easy for us in the arena of a strength. When a new situation calls for our strengths, our brain engages quickly. We perceive fast, learn a new skill or new knowledge, and integrate that learning immediately.

♠   Our natural strength surfaces quickly when we face a challenge. Without even thinking, it shows up.

STEP ONE: LIST ALL POSSIBLE STRENGTHS

Michael was unsure about completing the Clifton StrengthsFinder instrument. He didn't need someone else to tell him his strengths! He thought he could do a pretty good job on his own, so he began his quest by listing what he excelled in. Reviewing his calendar, he considered the last two weeks, noting which activities he really enjoyed, and which ones he hurried to get through. He followed the "Your Core Strengths" model and listed his strengths, what he does well, and what he loves:

♠   Developing salespeople.

♠   Interacting with customers, including irate ones.

- ♠ Solving problems for customers.
- ♠ Getting Joe, my senior VP, to agree to my ideas.
- ♠ Skiing.
- ♠ Fly-fishing.
- ♠ Turning around poor performers.
- ♠ Finishing projects around the house.
- ♠ Closing sales.
- ♠ Coaching my daughter's soccer team.
- ♠ Staying fit—getting to the gym.
- ♠ Talking with strangers.
- ♠ Being creative in my approach to managing sales meetings.
- ♠ Growing the perfect tomato, which I've been working on for eight years.
- ♠ Local politics.

He then took his list to a colleague, who added to it:

- ♠ Smoothing over conflicts.
- ♠ Making people laugh.
- ♠ Caring about people, especially his team.

Though it was a little embarrassing to ask for feedback and hear about his strengths, Michael was secretly delighted! It pleased him to know that others saw he cared and that he made people laugh. He decided to ask his wife and his best friend outside of work to add their insights. He compiled a great list!

Step Two: Uncover Themes

Before long, Michael realized that working with this expanding list of talents was becoming more confusing than clarifying. He began searching for themes and patterns. As he studied his own data and information from others—including a 360-degree assessment and prior performance reviews—common themes emerged and he drafted this list of core strengths:

- ♠ Developing others.
- ♠ Having fun; making people laugh.
- ♠ Talking with anyone and everyone.
- ♠ Caring.
- ♠ Getting things accomplished (once I set my mind to it).

Now Michael was curious—with his new list of strengths, he was ready to see what the Clifton StrengthsFinder™ told him. He completed the assessment and received his report immediately via e-mail. Michael summarized the results of his assessment and his top five strengths in this way:

1. "Maximizer": Focuses on strengths as a way to stimulate personal and group excellence. Seeks to transform something strong into something superb.

2. "Learner": Has a great desire to learn and continuously improve. In particular, the process of learning, rather than the outcome, excites a learner.

3. "Activator": Makes things happen by turning thoughts into action; often impatient.

4. "WOO" (Winning Others Over): Loves the challenge of meeting new people and winning them over. Derives satisfaction from breaking the ice and making a connection with people.

5. "Developer": Recognizes and cultivates the potential in others. Spots the signs of each small improvement and derives satisfaction from these improvements.

Michael noticed quite a bit of alignment between the strengths he defined and the list of strengths from the Clifton StrengthsFinder. This was a good start!

Step Three: Name the Game You'll Play

Now that Michael had a handle on his strengths, he realized he needed to remember them easily, so he could develop and maximize them. He knew he would remember his strengths better if he put them in his own words. He created this list and description of his strengths:

♠ Initiating—I turn thoughts into action.

♠ Developing others—I help others grow and develop.

♠ Influencing—I win others over.

♠ Learning—I acquire knowledge and learn fast.

♠ Amplifying—I transform something (or someone!) from good to great.

Yes! Those words seemed to capture the spirit of his strengths rather well! Notice that Michael's strengths are not simply his skills, such as fly-fishing, closing sales, or talking with strangers. Michael skillfully translated his initial list of skills and passions into core strengths—the innate talents and gifts that underpin his skills and passions. The skills of developing sales people, turning around poor performers, and coaching his daughter's soccer team transformed into the strength of "developing others." Likewise, closing sales and WOO became "influencing."

Step Four: Observe Yourself — Confirm Your Strengths

After Michael acknowledged that these strengths seemed fairly accurate, he sat down one Friday afternoon and listed his career successes and moments when he was particularly happy. As he reviewed the list, he began to answer the question, "What did I do to make those particular situations so successful?"

As he reflected on his successes from high school, college, and during the first 12 years of his career, he began to see the way his strengths had played out. He remembered when he first joined B2B Printers. While B2B had a fairly effective sales process at the time, he

51

thought he could make it better. Michael saw a few holes and several tangible opportunities for improvement, so early in his career he made a bold proposal to senior management to change the sales process. Much to his surprise, they accepted his proposal, kick-starting his career at B2B.

Michael also noticed his ability to close sales with difficult customers—customers that other salespeople, including senior executives, could not induce to buy. There was something about his communication with customers that allowed him to sway even the most entrenched positions and ultimately close the deal. Michael now recognized this as the strength of influencing. He also remembered that when he ran for office, he was elected easily to his college student council. Michael realized that he had the strength of winning others over as a student and early in his career. This strength was part of his life, not just his work.

During his Friday self-assessment, Michael also noted where he was not successful. For example, he'd always been weak at sales reporting. Though he attended workshops on data tracking and reporting, as well as time management courses, he only seemed to improve for a few weeks following each course. It was like losing weight. Everyone he knew who struggled with their weight complained about losing and then sliding back. Michael realized that he didn't like paperwork, data recording, or time management for a good reason—they were not his strengths. Michael's Friday afternoon musings made him much clearer about his strengths *and* his weaknesses.

Now eager to hear his boss Jane's input on his strengths, Michael showed her his list. Jane remarked, "These strengths look pretty good to me—do they feel right to you?" Michael said yes, but he wasn't quite sure about "developing others" and "learning." Even though he has a staff, he didn't see himself developing them very much. He gave them tools to support effective sales, but he didn't focus on coaching his people, nor did he intentionally work with them on specific development initiatives. Jane laughed! She had a different perspective! She saw sales associates who struggled to perform effectively go to work for Michael and begin to shine under his leadership. They were diamonds in the rough, and Michael seemed to soften their edges, making them much more effective. Michael viewed his efforts as simply putting together a good process. Like a fish in water, this is a classic case of being so immersed in the sea of our own strengths that we don't recognize a strength for what it is! In truth, it turns out Michael combines his strength of developing others and the strength he calls amplifying, which allows him to see and enhance the strengths of his staff members. He changed his definition of "developing others" to "I grow and develop others, especially their strengths!"

Michael still didn't clearly see how the strength of learning showed up in his work and personal life. He decided to trust the process, though, and to simply observe himself through time and watch for this strength to play out.

Michael noticed something interesting in his original list of strengths and passions. Wherever his passions and strengths overlap, he has been very successful, from closing deals to coaching his daughter's soccer team to solving customer problems. For example, Michael was passionate for local politics. He was successful in stumping for grassroots initiatives and influencing local stakeholders because he used his influencing strength. Yet, he experienced only mediocre success last year when he signed up to manage the money for a raffle benefiting the local food pantry. He had little opportunity to apply his strengths of amplifying, learning, initiating, influencing, or developing others in a number-crunching role. His contribution in no way aligned with his strengths. Michael was frustrated about being stuck in a trailer counting money when all the "fun" was happening outside at the ticket sales booth! As he assessed his strengths, he realized, again, that he creates the biggest opportunity for success when he integrates his strengths with his passions.

Most important to Michael, he realized that his strengths were not about what he does, but about who he is. He saw this only after making a list of his strengths, gathering feedback from others, looking for the themes and, now, observing his own actions. The steps in this process nudged him to a critical point—understanding the difference between who he is and what he *does*. Michael's strengths are all about who Michael *is*. Your strengths, too, are about who you are, not just what you do.

Further, Michael began to see that he could choose to apply his strengths to his passions in other areas of his life as well as work. Michael progressed on his journey of learning about his strengths while talking with a couple of his sales associates about their strengths. He could name the strengths of his staff much better than they could, driving home the point that our individual and unique combination of strengths really is our skin. He also began to see that he was so enjoying the learning process—the discovery and articulation of his strengths—that this must be a manifestation of his learning strength after all!

STEP FIVE: DESIGN YOUR LEADERSHIP BRAND

Throughout the next week or two as he worked with his boss, sales associates, and sales managers, Michael became more intrigued about the relationship of his strengths to his leadership. He remembered hearing about how leaders bring their own unique combination of strengths, passions, gifts, and purpose to the workplace, a combination that coalesces into a unique leadership style or a leadership brand. It's quite similar to how, for centuries, ranchers have marked their livestock with a unique brand, a symbol to differentiate one owner's cattle from another when they graze on common land. Branding, as we know it in the marketing context today, has its roots in this practice. Businesses pinpoint their unique differentiator, and create a brand or symbol as an image of their product or service, reflecting that differentiation, just as ranchers still today create unique symbols to distinguish their animals.

Applying strengths to our leadership is one of the most important and influential ways to manifest our strengths.

Leaders who lead from this place of strength also become more authentic and real as leaders. Noted Harvard Professor Robert E. Quinn

Throughout history, people had little need to know their strengths. A person was born into a position and a line of work; the peasant's son would be a peasant, the artisan's daughter an artisan's wife, and so on. But now people have choices. We need to know our strengths in order to know where we belong.
—Peter Drucker

writes that we can define and enter the fundamental state of leadership—the place where we do our best as leaders—when we rely on ourselves. Quinn says, "When leaders do their best work, they don't copy anyone. They draw on their own values and capabilities."[3]

Watching you tap into your authentic, real, and powerful self, and leading from that place, is inspiring to others. To you, it may feel daunting at first, but stick with it because, with time and attention, you'll learn to trust your core strengths and enrich your leadership.

Leadership not only calls forth our best strengths, it also causes us to externalize them, that is, to make them visible to others. Michael, for example, has "learning" as a strength, which is, for him, an internal strength. This strength is not very visible to others. That's part of the reason he had difficulty seeing and acknowledging this strength. When Michael identified his leadership strengths—his unique leadership brand—he saw that initiating, developing others, and influencing are the strengths he uses most.

Michael reflected further on his own leadership by asking himself these questions:

♠ Which of my strengths manifest when I lead?

♠ Which influence and inspire others?

- ♠ Which do I want to leverage more?
- ♠ Which could I hone and become even better at?
- ♠ Which inspire me?

A leadership brand is a simple statement of your unique strengths as a leader. It works for you as an overarching theme—a mantra, a guiding principle—as you capitalize on your strengths to lead others. Michael played with the words that describe his leadership strengths until he designed his leadership brand: "I attract, develop, and inspire others to action." Now that Michael knows his leadership brand, in every leadership situation, he looks for and creates opportunities to use these strengths. He integrates his strengths into all the actions he takes as a leader. This consistent focus on his strengths builds his credibility and success as a leader.

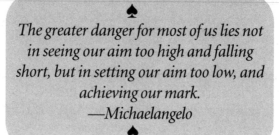

♠

The greater danger for most of us lies not in seeing our aim too high and falling short, but in setting our aim too low, and achieving our mark.
—Michaelangelo

♠

So, what can you learn from Michael? The exercises at the end of the chapter help you name your unique strengths. As you complete this process, you'll begin to have a sense, deep inside, that, "This is right, I have come home. I've found the keys to my success."

The Burden of Strengths Knowledge

Acute knowledge of our strengths is a blessing, yes, but it also can be a burden. When we know our strengths intimately, and can make informed choices about our work and our lifestyle, we create a life that is effective, passionate, and joyful. We hold the key to deep satisfaction.

And with this great knowledge also comes great responsibility. The burden we bear is this: How can I know my core strengths and not act upon that knowledge? How can I stay in a job, role, or commitment that does not make room for my strengths? How can I possibly pursue a path that discounts my strengths?

Unfortunately, some people move through life in ruts, operating on autopilot rather than proactively taking charge. They make choices that keep them in those ruts, clinging to the easy way and taking the path of least resistance. They hang on to old habits, stay on the known path for security, accept mediocrity, settle into complacency, become indifferent, and fully inhabit the comfort zone.

On the positive side, with strengths knowledge, we assume the responsibility to maximize, develop, and relentlessly pursue our strengths. Once we know and understand our strengths, how can we not act on them? With knowledge of our strengths, we can intensify the attention we place on our passions and interests. We become willing to be accountable for our work and life outcomes. There is no other course, and other paths fall to the side. Our paths—our destinies, our legacies—becomes immediately clearer as we take the five gems from the box and hold our individual diamond, sapphire, emerald, opal, and ruby as our own unique and personal gifts.

Unfortunately, that's not the way it happens for most of us. Maybe we start out in a career that doesn't make good use of our strengths. Maybe we fail before we begin to acknowledge and recognize our strengths. We try things on. We experiment. We play at different skills, opportunities, and roles. This isn't all bad. It's interesting, and may open up new pathways for us. However, we could reduce the pain and frustration if we learned about our strengths earlier. Similar to the Olympic ping-pong champion, rather than focusing on mastering our backhand, which we would never actually accomplish, we could focus on mastering our forehand (our strength), and become Olympic caliber in our career, in our leadership, and in our lives.

Bold Action

Terry, one of our leadership coaching clients, was not very happy with his relationship with his boss. No matter what he said or did, Terry never seemed to be able to please his boss. As director of training and development for a technology company, Terry excelled at his performance metrics. He built a highly motivated team and created programs that were well accepted by his customers. Yet, he couldn't seem to have a positive conversation with his boss. He watched his peers manage the politics much better—telling the boss what she wanted to hear, and agreeing to do things her way when they knew it wasn't the best way. Eventually, one of them gave Terry a valuable piece of feedback. On a flight home from an important and particularly frustrating meeting, the insensitive (but wise) colleague said, "Terry, you stink at managing politics."

Terry laughed! For the first time, he saw his weakness—and in an instant he saw his strengths just as clearly. He knew he needed to work for someone who valued what he could contribute to the organization—creativity, customer focus, and a passion for the development of individuals and organizations. He knew it was risky to leave—his pay was high and his responsibilities were broad—and yet Terry's core strengths of creativity, individual development, and strategy formulation were not valued in his current organization. Terry saw that using his strengths would lead to more success and internal peace. Terry left the organization and moved on to a highly successful career where he is valued for his strengths and not discounted for his alleged weaknesses.

Maturing Into Our Strengths

Learning about our strengths is similar to Terry's discovery. No one left them on the kitchen table when we became adults. Hopefully, we all have a sense of some of our strengths when we first enter the workforce. Our first job may leverage one or two of our most notable strengths. As we mature, we acquire more information about the variety and depth of our strengths. For example, if you took a job as a customer service rep for a company that makes cell phones, you may learn that you are good at listening to customers and, thus, can design solutions to their problems. You may soon realize that because of your strength in listening to customers, you excel at reading the market and predicting the best product and services to develop. You then discover that this strength encourages customer loyalty due to their satisfaction with the product mix. As your career evolves, and you continue to discover new strengths—and learn more about the depth and affect of each of them—you are able to use and leverage them more effectively, paving the way for greater success.

Notice the subtlety of these stories and what happens when we become clearer about our strengths: Our career choices actually become broader! If my strengths are to listen and influence, I can experience the joy of using these strengths in a huge variety of circumstances, situations, jobs, and careers. I am no longer stuck in my first career choice. Remember, our strengths are not what we do—but who we are. We can apply our unique configuration of strengths in nearly every industry, in government, or in a community organization.

As you can see, because strengths are broad and deep, our options in all dimensions of our lives expand when we know our core strengths. We can choose how we apply our strengths. Do I choose to use my strengths in business? In a volunteer capacity? Among my family members? To consider a new career? Actually, it's hard *not* to use our strengths in every capacity! Strengths inspire us to choose jobs and roles that truly maximize our performances, our excellences, and our successes.

Ah-Ha! in the Kitchen

People often ask Andrea how she became interested in strengths. The story is one of growing self-awareness.

I completed a leadership instrument that taught me a bit about who I am. Like any number of self-knowledge tools, this particular instrument helped me see my preferences, my view of the world, and how I position myself in my work. Having long been interested in self-discovery,

I've completed many similar instruments. I became truly intrigued about strengths later that evening, during one of those ah-ha moments in the kitchen, drinking a glass of wine and cooking dinner with my husband.

As I was talking about what I learned, I suddenly saw my strengths, clear as day! There's a very distinct pattern of traits, characteristics, qualities—ultimately, core strengths—that I could see unmistakably when I laid the self-awareness tools side-by-side. In that moment, I saw my unique combination of strengths. With that knowledge, I began to shift everything…how I did my work…what I said yes to and what I said no to…my volunteer activities…what I integrated into my life…what I eliminated from my life. In short, I began to answer the question, "How do I set myself up to be enormously successful and satisfied?" The answer is to recognize, acknowledge, claim, apply, and develop my strengths.

There are many tools available to gain this level of self-awareness. Certainly self-assessment instruments commonly used in business, such as the Myers-Briggs Type Indicator or the Enneagram, help us get a new view on our strengths. We also learn about our strengths by objectively looking at our successes. In what situations do we succeed? In what situations do we feel satisfied and fulfilled? In what situations do we feel uncomfortable, on edge, or out of our element? These questions give you clues to your strengths and your weaknesses, and because we are so accustomed to exploring our weaknesses, a little shift of focus will sharpen and clarify our evolving sense of our essential strengths.

There are woefully few instruments today that measure our strengths. However, we recommend two assessments wholeheartedly. The Clifton StrengthsFinder is a great tool to help you identify and clarify your strengths. It is the tool that most strength-focused leadership coaches use. It has an organizational context and business language infused within. It's a particularly effective tool for those of you who are leading in an organization.

Another instrument, less organizationally based, is simple to complete and quite interesting to use as a lens for exploring your strengths. Based on the work of Dr. Martin Seligman, the tool is called the VIA Signature Strengths Questionnaire. As of this writing, it's free. To take the instrument, go to *www.authentichappiness.org*. This quick questionnaire gives you your top five strengths, your "Signature Strengths," using everyday language. You'll see familiar words, such as humility, joyful, playful, and passionate. This easy-to-take questionnaire will give you a first pass, a glimpse, into your strengths.

Dealer's Choice

Congratulations! You know your strengths, and you've designed your leadership brand. You've named the game you'll play. You may not know every strength you possess, but you can speak to your top five or six strengths, notice where you are using them, and understand how they affect your work and life.

Implementation Ideas

Let's begin by reviewing the steps that Michael completed so that he could name his strengths. You can download a "Discover-Your-Strengths" worksheet with all five steps, at our Website, *www.play2yourstrengths.com*.

STEP 1: LIST ALL POSSIBLE STRENGTHS

List all your possible strengths and skills. Also list your passions. Some useful questions to ask yourself are:

- ♠ What do I excel at?
- ♠ What is easy for me?

♠ What do I enjoy?

♠ What am I passionate about?

For the next two weeks, keep track of activities that you enjoy, that you find fulfilling, *and* that make you feel strong; add these to your list. Also, ask others who know you well to add to your list. Be sure to include people from all walks of life—family, friends, and community connections—as well as people you work with every day. Ask people who will be open and honest with their answers. Four or five individuals will give you a good start on your strengths list.

STEP 2: UNCOVER THEMES

Complete a few tools, such as the Clifton StrengthsFinder and the VIA Signature Strengths Questionnaire to help you put names to your strengths and provide another lens on your list of strengths.

Group your strengths into "buckets" or categories that represent your deepest and most powerful strengths. Assign a working "theme" to each bucket.

To complete the Clifton StrengthsFinder, purchase a book that supplies you with a code for taking the instrument one time. You can buy the latest book , *StrengthsFinder 2.0,* by Tom Rath, from Gallup (Gallup Press, 2007) or, *Now, Discover Your Strengths* by Marcus Buckingham and Donald O. Clifton (Free Press, 2001).

The easy-to-take VIA Signature Strengths Questionnaire is free, simple, and identifies what the positive psychology folks call "character strengths." It helps to round out the strengths profile for many of our clients. (*www.authentichappiness.org* or *www.viastrengths.org.*)

STEP 3: NAME THE GAME YOU'LL PLAY

Even if you are not 100-percent certain you've created the perfect list of your strengths, go ahead and name them. Try to create no more than five named strengths so you can remember them and work with them. Naming your strengths is an important step. Assigning a name to a strength makes that strength more tangible and real, easier to access than a strength that is loose, unclear, and amorphous.

Memorize your strengths so you can easily begin to assess each new opportunity against your strengths.

STEP 4: OBSERVE YOURSELF

Throughout a two-to-four week period, notice where you excel. Notice, too, when you become engaged, enthused, excited, inspired, intrigued, or passionate! These purely emotional reactions are important because they offer clues to your deepest strengths.

Ask yourself these questions:

♠ Which of these strengths give me deep joy?

♠ Which strengths are fun to use?

♠ What strength am I most inspired to use?

♠ What strength is most interesting and intriguing to me?

Adjust your named strengths; rename them as needed so they sound right.

STEP 5: DESIGN YOUR LEADERSHIP BRAND

As a leader, consider how your strengths manifest themselves through your leadership. The application of our strengths to leadership is one of the most important and influential applications of our strengths.

Consider the strengths you listed in Step Four and ask yourself:

♠ Which of these strengths manifest when I lead?

♠ Which influence and inspire others?

♠ Which do I want to leverage more?

♠ Which could I hone and become even better at?

♠ Which inspire me?

Make note of these and lead from that place, integrating your strengths into all the actions you take as a leader.

For a real boost to your personal self-awareness and self-esteem, send an e-mail to 20 or 30 of your staff, clients, colleagues, and good friends that reads: "I am doing some work to identify my personal strengths and 'leadership brand.' I would appreciate your input! Please take a minute and, by return e-mail, tell me the three or four words that you believe describe the essence of me."

What you hear back—the patterns you see, similar and identical words, may put a completely new spin on how you describe your brand. And the e-mails will delight you!

Finally, create a leadership brand statement such as Michael did: "I attract, develop, and inspire others to action." Visit our Website for a helpful tool. Use your own words and your own unique description of how you lead others from your core strength. You may want to create a logo as well, a graphic representation of your leadership brand. Do whatever works to remind you to capitalize on your strengths as you lead others. This is the game you play, when you are playing at your best! And it is your unique leadership brand.

GIVE YOURSELF A TREAT

Complete the easy-to-take VIA Signature Strengths© Questionnaire. It's free, it's simple, and it identifies what the Positive Psychology folks call "character strengths." It helps to round out the strengths profile for many of our clients. (*www.authentichappiness.org* or *www.viastrengths.org*)

Another interesting assessment is the Kolbe A, found at *www.kolbe.com*. The Website described the assessment as a measure for your natural instincts—defining what you will or won't do.

Howard Gardner's work in multiple intelligences, originally developed and applied to children, provides an additional perspective on strengths. Check out the assessment tool offered by Literacy Works, at *http://literacyworks.org/mi/home.html*.

FLOW AND AUTHENTICITY

If you are unfamiliar with the concept of "flow," you might be intrigued by this book by the expert: *Flow: The Psychology of Optimal Experience* by Mihaly Csikszentmihalyi (Harper Perennial, 1990).

For an intriguing book about authenticity, read *True North: Discover Your Authentic Leadership* by Bill George, former Medtronic CEO and current Harvard Business School professor, and Peter Sims (Jossey-Bass, 2007).

CHAPTER THREE
DISCARDS:
KNOWING WHEN TO
HOLD 'EM OR FOLD 'EM

Discards: In a draw poker game, discards are cards you remove from your hand to make room for better cards and a stronger hand.

The poker game Seven-Card Stud is an excellent vehicle for exploring the nature of our weaknesses; each player receives seven cards, and from them the player must choose the five cards that create the strongest poker hand, discarding two. Imagine if you will, that these five best cards are your strengths, and the two worst cards your weaknesses. Easy so far, right?

Play begins with the dealer dealing two cards face down to each player at the table. Bets are placed based on the promise of those two cards.

Next, four cards are dealt face up, one at a time, to each player, with betting occurring throughout. Each player now has six cards: four showing and two hidden. Finally, each player is dealt one more card—the seventh card—face down. The kitty builds as players throw in chips based on their prospects!

It's like any other field: you have to develop yourself and your game. Poker is a skill, it's an art, it's a science. You have to improve continually and know your own weaknesses.
—*Alfred Alvarez*

The best possible poker hand is a royal flush: an ace, king, queen, jack, and 10 of the same suit. So, as long as it's our story, let's assume that you are dealt a royal flush—the strongest of all possible hands!

Let's watch your hand as each card appears. Your first two cards, dealt face down, are a four of hearts (4♥) and a queen of spades (Q♠). That doesn't tell you much—not until you can see more cards. The next four cards, dealt face up, are the 10, jack, and king of spades (10♠/J♠/K♠) and the two of diamonds (2♦). Hmmm, looks intriguing...you are well on your way to a superb hand!

Finally, the last card is dealt to you face down. You slowly lift the edge and take a hopeful look. You suppress a giggle and try to maintain a poker face! Your seventh card is—you guessed it—the ace of spades (A♠). Wow! What a hand! The strongest hand possible! You bid appropriately and finally have the opportunity to reveal your hand. Your table mates are awed when they see your royal flush in spades—10♠/J♠/Q♠/K♠/A♠—and you rake in a hefty pot! Can't do any better than that!

Such a strong hand is extremely rare in poker—but in real life, when we consider that each of us has been dealt the perfect mix of personal and professional strengths, we realize we all were dealt a royal flush!

Now, let's revisit our Seven-Card Stud hand again. Remember that the 4♥ was dealt face down and the 2♦ was dealt face up. The royal flush represents your five strengths and the 2♦ and 4♥ are your weaknesses. Makes sense. To play your strongest hand in the professional world, you want the royal flush—your strengths—visible. You want to play them frequently, have others see them at work, and design your life so these strong cards are always called into play. At the same time, you want to turn face down the 4♥ and the 2♦. Because these weaknesses are part of the hand you've been dealt in life, they can be acknowledged and put aside, if not discarded altogether. Because you have the opportunity to choose the five cards you play, why would you choose anything but your five strongest cards?

The World's Best Cyclist

Lance Armstrong—premiere cyclist, seven-time winner of the Tour de France, and celebrated cancer survivor—knows how to discard.

Before becoming the world's best cyclist Lance was an enthusiastic triathelete competing in running, swimming, and cycling. He was a good swimmer and fast on his feet as a runner, but he truly excelled at cycling. Recognizing that biking was his strength, Lance chose to concentrate his efforts on cycling competitions. His payoff is historic—literally as well as figuratively! In 1991, Lance played to his best strengths, won the U.S. amateur cycling championship and turned professional the following year. In 2002, *Sports Illustrated* named him Sportsman of the Year in honor of his fourth Tour de France win, and in recognition of his extraordinary perseverance in battling testicular cancer. For three years, Lance continued to improve his skill and enhance his strength, and in July of 2005, Lance Armstrong became the first cyclist to win the Tour de France seven consecutive times.

Lance discarded his weaker sports, running, and swimming, and focused all of his energy on developing his greatest strength—cycling. We can discard our personal weaknesses just as Lance did.

Similar to the discards in a poker game, we can throw away most of our weaknesses and defer to our stronger cards, making us more successful and competitive. Discarding a weakness is an excellent strategy because few of us will ever be stellar or world-class in a true weakness. Mediocre or adequate performance is possible, but superior achievement in an area of weakness is highly unlikely.

Because of society's myth of well-roundedness, we learn early in life to try to overcome all of our weaknesses. We're told to concentrate and apply ourselves even if we don't enjoy it. We're taught that if we just "try harder" we can overcome our weakness. How utterly exhausting and frustrating! Attempting to overcome a weakness takes time, commitment, and effort. The truth of the matter is, few weaknesses must be overcome. Most of our weaknesses can simply be managed. It's easier and less painful to manage a weakness than to attempt to overcome it through extensive training, education, and practice. When faced with this radical idea, many clients ask, "But how do I know if a weakness must be overcome, or if I can manage it so it doesn't get in the way?"

An excellent question! Our intention in this book is to shift leaders away from an obsession with weaknesses, we hesitated to write a chapter on this subject. However, we recognize that we'd be remiss to completely ignore weaknesses, because we've all been taught from the first day of school that overcoming them is an admirable goal. The compelling reason we've included this chapter is because understanding our weaknesses will help us clearly see our strengths! Knowing your weaknesses provides a frame of reference for knowing your strengths.

Discarding Your Weak Cards

As we learned from Lance, discerning and managing our weaknesses can be the most important step we take toward making the most of our strengths. Creating a simple plan to manage our weakness frees us to capitalize on our strengths and develop them further. How effective would Lance be in the Tour de France if he split his training effort by preparing for running, swimming, and cycling? In sports, in poker, and in work we need to assess our strengths and play to them—but also to understand our weaknesses—our areas of vulnerability—so we can compensate for them, discard them if possible, and put our efforts into fully realizing our strengths and their potential.

Just as important, knowing your weaknesses shows you where *not* to put your energy. Instead of creating personal growth and development plans that are 90-percent designed to overcome weakness and 10-percent designed to maximize strengths, as we've historically done, imagine what would happen if we reversed the percentages and concentrated the majority of our growth and learning on our strengths. Wow! This alternative approach makes development intriguing, exciting, and compelling. If we focus on learning more about our strengths and how to apply them, we actually create more energy and higher confidence, improving our performance and our satisfaction.

Throughout the years we've noticed that many leadership professionals in human resources and training functions shun the word "weakness" as though a weakness is something to be avoided at all costs…a scourge to its owner. We believe it's time to admit we all have weaknesses. When we know our weaknesses, we also know the intellectual, mental, physical, and emotional situations in which we will not excel. Great! We don't want to struggle to perform our best or lead from those no-win situations. Instead, let's search for the situations that make the most of our strengths.

Unfortunately, these same leadership professionals want to replace the word *weakness* with the misguided phrase *development opportunity*. This is precisely the mentality that needs to change, not only in our workplaces, but in our high schools and colleges as well. Simply because a skill or ability is limited does not mean it presents a development opportunity. We are not destined to achieve perfection in every single skill or task we undertake. We can, however, choose to use our gifts and talents to the best of our ability. If I'm not good at design, why focus my development time, money, and energy on becoming an architect? Let me hire one instead—one who is using his gifts, talents, and strengths to contribute his best to the world.

When we assume all of our weaknesses require improvement, we buy into the myth of well-roundedness. If we are excited and intrigued to learn a new skill, even if it doesn't play to our strengths, that's great! But when we address a weakness that bores us or is uninspiring, we waste considerable effort, and eventually become discouraged and frustrated. We need to assess if it's worth it to improve on a weakness, to prevent us from wasting our precious resources of money, time, and energy.

Once we rivet our attention on weakness, we exaggerate everything that works against us. We blind ourselves to real strengths and cannot recognize, much less use, what we actually have going for us.
—Deborah Kolb and Judith Williams

Two Types of Weaknesses: Low-Impact and High-Impact

In *Now, Discover Your Strengths*, Marcus Buckingham and Donald O. Clifton define weakness as "anything that gets in the way of excellent performance." That definition can cover a lot of weaknesses! Everything from height to geography to disinterest in moon rocks could be a weakness in a particular job or profession. Yet, we also know that some weaknesses matter more than others. How do we decide which of our weaknesses (if any) need special attention?

How do we know if working to improve a particular weakness is worth the time and effort? To answer these questions, we need to identify our weaknesses, decide if any inhibit our performance or keep us from fully applying our strengths, and assess which ones can be managed or discarded. Let's explore two distinct types of weaknesses we all face: low-impact (inconsequential weaknesses), and high-impact (career-limiting weaknesses).

LOW-IMPACT WEAKNESS

A low-impact weakness is simply a part of our make up. This inconsequential weakness poses no real threat because it has little effect on our lives. Its irrelevance to our excellent performance means we can "discard" it.

Low-impact weaknesses are relatively easy to manage. Once we acknowledge the weakness, we can create and implement a strategy to deal with it. If I am weak at the logic behind creating spreadsheets, I would be wise to choose a job in which creating spreadsheets isn't a significant requirement! If I occasionally need to create a spreadsheet, then I can find an administrative assistant, colleague, or someone in the organization to do it for me. A simple and effective way to manage a weakness is to find someone who can easily compensate for it and create an agreement with him to do so.

For example, one of Andrea's low-impact weaknesses is coordination in mechanical endeavors. (Translation: she's a bit of a klutz!) She is not very adept at using tools and experiences high frustration and limited success when she tries to do so. Because she really has no desire to improve in this area, she asks her husband to do mechanical things. Recognizing her husband's limitations as well, she also hires an auto mechanic and brings in plumbers and electricians when needed. These people are good! They have strengths and aptitudes that align with the task; that's how they earn their living! As a leadership development consultant and executive coach, Andrea recognized her weakness and chose a career that does not call for mechanical aptitude! For this insignificant weakness, she developed a weakness management plan.

73

HIGH-IMPACT WEAKNESS

The second type of weakness, the career-limiting type, more often than not proves formidable because it has a high impact. A high-impact weakness is the lack of knowledge, skill, or behavior essential to current or future performance in a role or career. It cannot simply be discarded or managed, because it has a direct bearing on career or life success. A career-limiting weakness must be improved, or it will affect our excellent performance in our current role. In some cases, a high-impact weakness may so limit one's career that the individual must choose a new career path. A student in training to become a nurse, who faints at the sight of blood, has encountered a career-limiting weakness. It can't be ignored or discarded. It needs attention. This high-impact weakness must be lessened, reduced, or curbed—or she must choose a new career. If we find ourselves in this awkward situation, we need to nudge ourselves from poor performance to the lofty place of mediocre performance.

A number of years ago, Andrea discovered she had a high-impact weakness. She wasn't very good at marketing. Unfortunately, because she already ran her own company, this lack of marketing savvy limited her business success. Of course, a certain amount of marketing can be outsourced; however, Andrea knew that before a business owner could hire marketing support, she must first establish a basic strategy and direction for the marketing efforts. Not wanting this high-impact weakness to limit her business, she learned the business of marketing. She talked to seasoned marketers, read books, studied, took notice of what intrigued her from a marketing perspective, and paid particular attention to what she didn't like. Eventually, Andrea learned enough about marketing to guide her business. She didn't become a marketing guru; she still hires partners to help her—marketing strategists and technicians who offset this weakness. The creative and effective presentation of benefits to a potential client will never be her strength. However, she learned enough—and became proudly mediocre in her marketing efforts—to sustain and grow a healthy, thriving business! She didn't overcome her career-limiting weakness, but she did manage it, and lessened its negative impact.

In the first example, with a low-impact weakness that is more of a nuisance than a genuine problem, Andrea created a plan to manage the weakness. In the second example, a high-impact career-limiting weakness, Andrea devised a method to lessen the weakness—to actually reduce it so the weakness didn't inhibit her performance or keep her from fully applying her strengths. This is a crucial distinction in weakness management. For a low-impact weakness, managing it means letting it go or corralling and using external resources. For a high-impact weakness, lessening the impact of the weakness means that we must improve, even just a bit, to achieve adequate performance. When we design our work to make the best use of our strengths, if we find we still have an important career-limiting weakness, then, and only then, will we need a plan to reduce the impact of that weakness. Let's start identifying your low-impact weaknesses, and discovering if you have a high-impact weakness.

Find Your Two of Diamonds and Four of Hearts

If you want to lead from your strengths, display them face up, and show your royal flush to the world, you also need to conceal your personal 2♦ and 4♥. Lay these face down, hide them, and downplay them. These weak cards do not help you when you want to play the strong hand you've been dealt. In Seven-Card Stud, it is easy to see which cards are weak cards. However, in life, to downplay and manage your weaknesses, you need to know what they are. Usually this poses no real difficulty, because we are typically quite aware of what we're not good at—primarily because we focus on it all too often.

To play to your strengths, create a list of your weaknesses. As with strengths, look for the things you don't like to do or don't do well, and also identify the missing skill or talent that underpins the tasks you don't like. In Chapter 2♠ when you identified your strengths, one place you looked for clues was in assessment instrumentation, such as the Clifton StrengthsFinder. Instruments of this type can help highlight your weaknesses. If you are a strong Intuitive, does that mean Sensing is a weakness? It might not be; it may just be something you'd prefer not to do. If you perceive Sensing as a true weakness, put it on your list. Consider weaknesses in your work and your personal life. Here are some useful questions to ask yourself to become clearer about your weaknesses:

- ♠ Have I been in a job that required skills or attributes that I did not possess?

- ♠ What do I procrastinate while doing at work or at home? (In addition to going to the dentist!)

- ♠ What do I shy away from?

- ♠ What do I agonize over? (We feel confident about our strengths, and unsure of ourselves in our weaknesses.)

- ♠ What isn't fun for me? (If you groan and moan and get crabby before you have to do it, it's probably not a strength!)

- ♠ When do I ask for help (or secretly wish you had a genius at your beck and call)?

- ♠ When does my inner critic kick in? ("Oh, self, I don't know why you agreed to make that presentation. You never make good presentations.")

- ♠ What causes my neck to get sore, my stomach to turn over, my eye to twitch, or my head to ache?

- ♠ What do I delegate? (You may delegate for development purposes, or you may delegate something you are just not good at. This is actually a strategy for managing a weakness—but more on that later.)

Do you have a skill weakness that could affect your success? Put it on your list. Perhaps you lack proficiency at mechanical activities. Put that on your list. Or perhaps you have a perspective or attitude that limits your effectiveness, such as being overly critical. Add this to your list, too.

Perhaps you don't know much about leadership. Or maybe you hate doing paperwork and procrastinate until it's past due. List these weaknesses—all of them—and don't get depressed! Remember clarity about your weaknesses creates clarity about your strengths. Take these weaknesses as simple facts about you. You aren't posting your weaknesses on the Internet or hanging them on your office door for all to see—though you may do so inadvertently if you don't acknowledge them. You are completing a thorough and honest analysis in order to maximize your success.

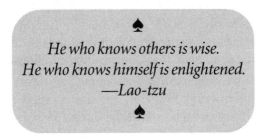

♠

He who knows others is wise.
He who knows himself is enlightened.
—Lao-tzu

♠

Many methods exist to get a clear handle on your weaknesses. Your staff, colleagues, boss, spouse, and customers might be delighted to help! You can also use a 360-degree instrument to gather anonymous feedback from work colleagues or ask them yourself. Conversations with others about your weaknesses offer an additional benefit: you increase your authenticity, thereby making your relationships more honest and building trust that creates a safe environment for both of you. When you talk openly with others about your weaknesses, you open yourself to better relationships.

Finally, particularly with work competencies that someone thinks are necessary, you might want to look for these clues to identify a weakness:

♠ You learn it slowly. It seems to take an inordinate amount of struggling and extra effort to "get" and apply the concepts.

77

♠ You are defensive about it. You may hear yourself talking about how you would be better at it, if only X occurred. "It's not that I'm a bad listener—it's just that Mary talks all around the topic and never seems to get to the bottom line." Or, "But I'm a good listener at home, even though my staff thinks I don't do so well at work."

♠ It lowers your confidence when you encounter a situation that requires you to use it. You may get an anxious feeling in your belly, or notice that running away and hiding sounds like a really great idea. A little success may feel good for a while, but ultimately you know you are not good at this task or skill, and the next time you encounter it, that familiar sinking feeling returns.

♠ You have no exciting and compelling future vision about this skill. Your vision about it is simply to master it well enough to make the sinking feeling go away. You don't find yourself daydreaming about how great you will be.

Are you feeling a little draggy and defeated now? It's not a surprise, because focusing on weaknesses makes us feel uninspired, depleting our energy and enthusiasm. If it doesn't feel good, it isn't a strength. While focus on strengths is crucial, identifying weaknesses is important so we can manage them. As leaders who recognize the need to grow, we may concentrate so much on overcoming a weakness that we lose our objectivity and become obsessive. The good news is that there are reasonable and rational ways to deal with both low-impact and high-impact weaknesses.

How to Manage a
Low-Impact Weakness

After you create your list of weaknesses, look specifically for those that are low-impact or inconsequential. These are weaknesses you can manage. Second, study the list for any high-impact or career-limiting weakness. And remember—you might not have any high-impact weakness! If you do find a high-impact weakness, accept that it must be lessened or reduced. Don't be discouraged—most of our weaknesses are low-impact because we naturally play to our strengths. Low-impact weaknesses can be managed easily by employing one of three strategies:

1. Delegate it.
2. Purchase it.
3. Ignore it.

Let's look at these in more detail.

Delegation is a critical skill. The only way to make your weakness irrelevant is to respect others' strengths and use them.
—*Warren Bennis*

STRATEGY ONE: DELEGATE IT

Strong and effective leaders know how important it is to compensate for their weaknesses when hiring staff. In his successful book *Good to Great* (Harper Collins Inc., 2001), Jim Collins documents a few surprising and interesting differentiators between the great companies and the merely good. One of them is, "First who...then what." In Collins' metaphor, the great companies put the right people "on the bus," and only then decide where to drive the bus.

As leaders, our first priority is to put the right people on our bus; then, engage their strengths, and delegate to them. Makes sense, doesn't it? You delegate what you're not good at. Delegate what you don't like to do. Delegate to those who not only perform the task better, but who do it with pride and commitment. When you find a task that doesn't fit with your strengths, look around. Someone would love to do it. Let him! He will shine!

Some leaders we coach are under the mistaken impression that they must be effective at every task they delegate. What a waste of talent and energy! It's not possible, and it certainly isn't an effective use of resources. We often hear leaders say, "I wouldn't ask others to do anything I wouldn't do myself." Well, why not? This statement doesn't make sense! Do you perform your own dental work?

The best strategy is to hire people with strengths that complement ours, and then delegate responsibility to them according to their strengths.

We know a training manager, Dan, who is a powerful and skilled stand-up facilitator, but who lacks skill in training design. And he knows it. So, he hires excellent designers, freeing himself for training delivery and, with the strength of his team, creates much better training than he would have done on his own.

Take a look at the low-impact weaknesses on your list and consider which of these could be delegated to someone on your team whom you can trust to do an excellent job. Now, go ahead, delegate it!

Strategy Two: Purchase It

There are many ways to "purchase" strengths in order to manage a weakness. The most obvious is hiring someone to do it for us. Successful organizations hire consultants and advisors to assist with an expertise that they do not possess in sufficient measure. A technology firm purchases marketing from an advertising agency. A homeowner hires a plumber to fix a leaky pipe. An entrepreneur hires an accountant to stay on top of tax requirements.

We can also purchase a strength to manage a weakness by developing an effective partnership. In this case, cash may or may not exchange hands. A good partnership occurs when someone assists you by compensating for your weakness while you compensate for his. Hospitals partner with physicians in the community to provide a broad array of medical services. Physicians partner with hospitals to provide the services and infrastructure they cannot. New entrepreneurs often partner with others who have greater access to particular clients and services. FedEx partners with contractors who run their own businesses, purchase their own vans and trucks, and deliver and pick up packages for FedEx. This highly effective partnership is symbiotic. FedEx could not deliver its value proposition to customers without the contractors, and the contractors would have far less business without FedEx creating the market.

An important distinction between partnering and purchasing is that, in partnering, you are a resource to the partnership because you add the value of your unique strengths. To prepare yourself to create an effective partnership, understand and articulate the value you add. If you are simply purchasing a service, the value you add to the relationship is the fee you pay for the service. In a partnership, the payoff is a quid pro quo. Partnerships can be exciting and intriguing. Most importantly, both partnerships and purchasing are essential tools to help us manage weaknesses and each has its place.

Our friend Walter is a brilliant songwriter who can teach us about effective partnerships. Walter earns his living facilitating teams in a manufacturing plant, but he hopes someday to make songwriting his profession. He also has a strong and powerful singing voice, a marvelous complementary skill to his songwriting. On the other hand, Walter's guitar skills stop at the opening bars of "Down in the Valley." One day over coffee, shortly after we began to work together implementing strengths-based leadership at his plant, Walter told us he was working hard learning to play the guitar, so he could effectively market and sell his songs. He struggled with this for a few months, having little fun and even less success. Eventually, Walter had an epiphany. He embarked upon a search to find someone to play back-up and discovered several talented local guitar players thrilled at the opportunity for greater exposure! Taking advantage of what he learned about strengths in our work together, Walter formed a mutually beneficial partnership with an excellent local musician who loves Walter's songs. The relationship is both complementary and symbiotic. The guitar player has an audience he would not otherwise have. Focusing on his strength liberates Walter from the frustrating and not-very-successful task of learning to play the guitar. With his time and energy concentrated on his strengths, Walter writes more—and better quality—songs.

So, take a long, honest, insightful, and liberating look at your low-impact weaknesses and ask yourself, what partnership can I create to buy the strength I need?

Think outside the box! Look in different directions, under rocks, and around corners. Your partner may be a colleague or someone you don't yet know in another department. There is an individual or an organization just waiting to partner with you! We guarantee it!

STRATEGY THREE: IGNORE IT

Sometimes we can simply ignore a weakness. If it is irrelevant to our path and our purpose, we just turn our back on it. This management strategy is often overlooked when a leader or a business owner puts together a development plan. Andrea well understands her weakness in things mechanical. It's a weakness she can easily ignore in her role as a consultant, coach, and writer. It simply doesn't matter.

To be sure, ignoring the weakness may mean negotiating for changed expectations with your boss, partner, or team—either when you take a job or perhaps later, when your role evolves. By learning more about our strengths and weaknesses, we create the leverage to negotiate our current role—or to negotiate a new role that allows us to rely on our strengths and manage our weakness. Can you give away a task that calls on your weakness, and still do an excellent job? Do you need to renegotiate expectations with your boss or a peer? Dan, the excellent facilitator (but poor designer), hired the skill of training design. He also may have been able to renegotiate his role with his boss. Utilizing an "ignore it" strategy, Dan could have offered to manage all the training delivery and none of the design. A colleague who excels in design may have been happy to support this adjustment! By renegotiating expectations, you create an opportunity to design a job in which you can play your strongest cards, take advantage of your strengths, and ignore your weaknesses.

How to Manage a
High-Impact Weakness

Sometimes, we do have a high-impact, career-limiting weakness for the career path we have chosen. Provided that the path is truly connected to our passions, values, and purposes, and it makes excellent use of our strengths, we may choose to lessen a weakness in order to perform at excellence.

For example, while many strengths can be well-utilized in a leadership role, some weaknesses are career-limiting for a leader. Research completed by Lominger Limited, publisher of *FYI: For Your Improvement: A Handbook Development and Coaching Guide*, indicates there are specific behaviors that can derail a leader's career. Lominger calls these behaviors "career stallers and stoppers." If one of these career stallers is characteristic of you and your leadership, you must moderate it or choose another path. A career staller will keep you from fully utilizing your strengths. Derailers differ slightly from role to role. Leaders can be derailed by a number of weaknesses, including:

♠ Being overly ambitious.

♠ Failing to establish and maintain effective relationships.

♠ Being unable to lead personal and organizational change.

- ♠ Micromanaging.
- ♠ Lacking self-knowledge.
- ♠ Possessing insufficient emotional intelligence.

What competencies are on your weakness list? Honestly ask yourself if any of these weaknesses can hurt your career. You may find your own boss or a trusted mentor can assist you in identifying any potential derailers. You may also choose to ask yourself these critical questions:

- ♠ Does my current career path make excellent use of my strengths?
- ♠ If so, do I have a weakness that keeps me from fully applying my strengths?
- ♠ Do I have a weakness that must be eliminated, mitigated, reduced, or curbed, so that it doesn't hold me back?

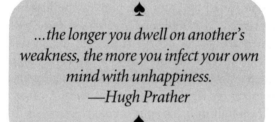

♠

...the longer you dwell on another's weakness, the more you infect your own mind with unhappiness.
—Hugh Prather

♠

- ♠ Can I lessen the impact of my weakness sufficiently to succeed and sustain success in my current career path?

Our client, Maggie, illustrates one way to mitigate a weakness. As vice president of organization development for a hospital conglomerate, Maggie was intrigued by the idea of strengths-based development. Intuitively, she saw that focusing on strengths would

84

inspire staff members to seek roles and responsibilities that provide significant opportunity to use and maximize their strengths, creating a win for the individual and for the organization.

Maggie also recognized that occasionally a career-limiting weakness does appear. For example, Maggie identified a director in the IT department, Jim, whose strengths clearly matched the role requirements in content, function, and leadership. However, Jim could not prepare or manage his budget—an imperative skill if he expected to move up in the organization.

To continue on his career path, Jim needed to address this career-limiting weakness. Maggie could not, in good conscience, support his development plan without including development in budget management.

Maggie asked the important question: "How can Jim use his strengths to help him deal with this weakness?" Maggie knew that one of Jim's strengths was logic. He understands cause and effect and rational thinking. She found a mentor who could teach Jim budget management by emphasizing cause and effect, explaining how dollars flow into and out of his department. Jim's face lit up because he was able to comprehend the logic of a budget process. Once he saw the logic, he successfully applied it to identifying future needs, assessing budget implications, planning and tracking expenditures, and making monthly budget projections. While Jim will likely never excel at budgeting, he clearly accepts that understanding his budget is a weakness, yet a necessity. Jim transformed his performance in budget management from inadequate to acceptable. Now he has enough ability to effectively manage his budget. Notice that Jim's plan to address his weakness revealed a "skill-in-waiting." Jim improved his skills, but he has not created a new strength. He has merely applied his strength of logic and analysis to a different venue—in this case, a budget.

Maggie understood that, to teach Jim the skill of budget management, she had to appeal to his natural strengths of logic and analysis. For another director, with strengths in empathy and relationship building, Maggie may have chosen to teach the skill of budgeting using games, or to use scenarios that highlight the people-related impact of a budget.

Jim's inability to manage his department's finances was a high-impact, career-limiting weakness. It began to restrict his opportunities because it depleted energy he could otherwise use to leverage his strengths. Managing a budget is not a core strength for Jim's role; rather, it's an ancillary skill the organization needs from him. If Jim were missing an important strength for his role, his career in that role would be cut short early on. An artist-in-training who learns the skills of brush strokes, shadow, and light, but who doesn't have the strength of creativity, will never go far as an artist, and likewise, a manager who cannot create relationships will fail. In both cases, these are primary strengths necessary to create excellence in these roles. Jim has the luxury of taking action to reduce the impact of his weakness. He is not attempting to create a brand new strength.

If you decide to address a weakness, you need to create a personal development plan with concerted and targeted efforts. Engage these development strategies:

- ♠ Ask yourself how your strengths can help you learn this skill.

- ♠ Expand your current role—or seek a new role—so you have the opportunity to both learn and practice the weakness in a safe setting.

- ♠ Set up a process to gather ongoing feedback on your effectiveness in this area, as you work to take the edge off your weakness.

- ♠ Work with a coach or mentor to mitigate the weakness.

- ♠ Acquire specific knowledge through training and reading.

In our work, we encounter leaders with an enormous capacity for arrogance. Some of these individuals sufficiently soften their arrogance and succeed as leaders. On the other hand, a different weakness—such as being nonstrategic—may tank an aspiring leader's career. You may not be able to lessen the impact of being nonstrategic. If you are more tactical than strategic, and it's getting in the way of your current role, you may need to look for a better match. To create a sustaining and fulfilling career, you may need to seek a role

♠

If I had a hammer
I'd hammer in the morning
I'd hammer in the evening...
All over this land.
—Pete Seeger

♠

that does not require a 30,000-foot view. If success in your current career or role depends upon excelling in one of your weaknesses, then you are, simply stated, in the wrong career.

Not Everything Is a Nail

We have eager clients who ask, "Is it possible to overuse my strength? Can my strength become a weakness by using it too much?" While we probably cannot "overuse" our strengths when aligned with responsibilities that call for it, we can "misuse" by using our strengths when it isn't needed. When the task is deciding among options, and the super-creative marketing director keeps throwing new ideas into the discussion, she's using a strength when needed. It's time for the strength of decision-making, even if she still has four new ideas! Because she's holding a hammer of strengths, she begins to see everything as a nail.

When she truly understands her strength, she will also understand when it isn't time for her to use it—when it's actually time for her to rely on others who have the strength of decision-making. Sometimes the best action is to make way for a person with that strength to jump in. Remember, no one has every strength. The myth of well-roundedness has us believing we should be good at everything. But we know we're not. No one is limitless!

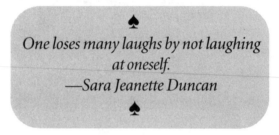

♠

One loses many laughs by not laughing at oneself.
—Sara Jeanette Duncan

♠

Weaknesses: Just for the Fun of It

The more-ambitious souls among us may choose to diminish a weakness just for the fun of it! For example, our client, Joan, isn't very good at learning languages. She painfully survived high school French. Trying to learn a language consistently lowers her self-confidence. Now that Joan recognizes her language weakness, and accepts the extra effort and occasional frustration learning a language will inevitably bring, she can choose to learn a language anyway, in spite of her weakness! Recently, Joan successfully completed three years of Spanish at her local community college. Was she a good student? Yes! Will she ever excel at Spanish? No! Joan accepts the fact that she will never be facile—and that's just fine. While she will never be hired by the United Nations as a Spanish interpreter, she learned enough to travel to Spanish-speaking countries and understand directions to "el baño." She is learning Spanish because she chooses to—not because she believes it will catapult her to the zenith of her career. Even with the frustration and self-doubt, she's having a blast learning Spanish.

How can a challenging and frustrating learning process be fun, let alone a blast? Well, this is the last point we want to make about weaknesses. Once you truly "grok" your strengths (a word borrowed from Martian according to Robert Heinlein, author of *Stranger in a Strange Land*. To grok is to gain an instant and deep spiritual understanding of something or to establish a rapport with somebody), you will find your weaknesses laughable! They become insignificant and funny. Joan now laughs at her struggles with the numerous conjugations of the Spanish verb *ser*.

She doesn't need to be profoundly proficient at everything she chooses to do. Because she takes advantage of her strengths, there are many avenues where Joan can shine. She can choose to build on a weakness—to move her proficiency all the way up to mediocre (or better)—for the sheer joy of it! There is no downside to approaching a weakness this way, and this fresh, new perspective on weaknesses is liberating!

One Final Strategy: Build a Round Team

We know it is not a viable strategy for us, as individuals, to even attempt to be completely "round"; that is, to have all skills at our fingertips. It is, however, a viable strategy to create a "round" team. Someone on the team may add the strength of innovation while someone else adds the ability to execute. One person on your team may excel at building relationships with customers while another may shine at product fulfillment. You may have strength in strategy formation and your right-hand person may excel at translating that strategy into actionable plans. A "round" team acts powerfully, building on each member's strengths and compensating for each other's weaknesses.

John Inglish, our client mentioned in Chapter 1♠, is a strong visionary and an effective strategist. He inspires others with his great dreams. He commits his time, passion, and energy to communicate his vision to those who excel at making it happen. He creates opportunities to use his strong hand to further his vision for his organization, his customers, and his legacy. He also knows his weaknesses and manages them by using team member strengths. The combination of individual strengths, coupled with weakness awareness, allows each person on John's "round" team to effectively apply his strengths, and only his strengths, to the situations he encounters and creates.

All leaders, no matter how lofty their titles, have room to expand and grow their strengths to create a more successful, powerful, and far-reaching impact. Stop wasting time on your weaknesses!

Do not try to teach a pig to sing – it wastes your time and irritates the pig!

Implementation Ideas

Ready to explore your weaknesses further? Because developing our strengths requires acknowledging and accepting our weaknesses, let's take a frank look at our weaknesses. Once we acknowledge and accept them, we can move on to the exciting challenge of working fully from our strengths. To be sure, many of us know the things we put off and the things we do not enjoy. Only rarely, though, do we admit they are actually weaknesses! So, in the safety and security of your home, office, or local coffee shop, grab a piece of paper and a cup of java, and settle in to create an implementation plan to address your weaknesses.

ASK OTHERS ABOUT YOUR WEAKNESSES

If you are unsure about your weaknesses, you can "make my day" for the people around you (thank you, Clint) by asking your spouse, colleagues, and best friends to answer the questions for you! Give them time to prepare so you receive a comprehensive list. Assure them you want their honest feedback, and prepare to receive it.

ASK YOURSELF ABOUT YOUR WEAKNESSES

These questions will help:
- ♠ What do you learn slowly?
- ♠ What are you defensive about?
- ♠ What lowers your confidence?
- ♠ For what do you have no exciting and compelling future vision?
- ♠ What do you procrastinate doing at work or at home?

- ♠ What do you shy away from?
- ♠ What do you agonize over?
- ♠ Have you been in a job that required skills or attributes that you did not possess?
- ♠ What isn't fun?
- ♠ When do you ask for help?
- ♠ When does your inner critic kick in?
- ♠ What causes your neck to get sore, your stomach to turn over, your eye to twitch, or your head to ache?
- ♠ What do you delegate?

LAUGH WITH, AND AT, YOURSELF!

When we look in the mirror we see our hair, our eyes, our noses, and our ears. Now imagine that, similar to seeing your physical reflection, you are able to see your weaknesses in a mirror. What do you notice? What stands out? Acknowledge and accept your weaknesses. Once you begin, you will be amazed at how little time it takes before you can laugh at those challenges and say, "I really am not very good at _____, and it shows!"

DELEGATE

List every task you'd like to delegate—whether it's trimming the hedges, managing your taxes, or dealing with employee conflicts. Identify the best person to whom you could delegate each task. If you had no concerns about money, resources, or quality, what would you like to delegate? What patterns do you see among the tasks you want to delegate? That pattern may be your weakness. Who in your organization loves these tasks? Go ahead—delegate!

GIVE UP PERFECTION

We are not destined to be perfect specimens of humanity. Let it go.

THINK OUTSIDE OF THE BOX!

What partnership can you create to buy the strength you need?

PICK ONE WEAKNESS TO IGNORE.

Practice ignoring it. Then pick another…and another.

DO YOU HAVE A HIGH-IMPACT WEAKNESS?

You might not! After you identify the low-impact weaknesses you can manage, is there anything left? Do you have one high-impact, career-limiting weakness? Consider carefully any traits critical to your role that show up on your weakness list, and ask yourself these important questions:

- ♠ Does my current career path make excellent use of my strengths?

- ♠ If so, do I have a weakness that keeps me from fully applying my strengths?

- ♠ Do I have a weakness that must be eliminated or mitigated or reduced or curbed—so that it doesn't hold me back?

- ♠ Can I lessen the impact of my weakness sufficiently to succeed and sustain success in my current career path?

How motivated are you to lessen your weakness, or to become at least mediocre in it? If you're motivated, put together a development plan. Use the following template to capture your goals and action steps. (You can download a copy at our Website, *www.play2yourstrengths.com*.)

Weakness	Low or high impact?	If low, delegate, purchase, or ignore it?	If high, what will it take?	By when?	What strengths help with this weakness?
1.					
2.					
3.					
4.					
5.					

READ LANCE ARMSTRONG'S INSPIRING AUTOBIOGRAPHY

It's Not About the Bike (Putnam, 2000) teaches us about Lance's few weaknesses and highlights his strengths.

The following chart shows how we can apply these strengths and learn about our weaknesses.

WORK WITH A COACH OR A MENTOR

If you decide that working with a coach is a good idea, put together a plan with your coach that helps you manage each of your inconsequential weaknesses, and bolster any career-limiting weakness to adequate performance.

Chapter Four

Showdown:

Playing for High

Stakes

Showdown: At the end of the final betting round, showdown is when all active players turn their cards face-up to see who has won the pot.

CNET News.com recently featured a story about two young entrepreneurs who were unable to acquire the venture financing needed to start their business, so they play poker online for 10 to 15 hours each week, netting enough to pay the bills and keep the cash flow churning.[1] It's extremely high-risk, but they have parlayed their poker skills into the cash needed to finance their dream. Now *that's* playing for high stakes!

Hopefully, you don't have to finance a fledgling business by playing amateur poker. However, you will encounter challenging situations at work and at home to which you want to bring your best strengths.

Becoming a More Potent Player

In spring 2007, (former) Vice President Al Gore's movie, *An Inconvenient Truth*—a passionate and inspirational look at global warming—won an Academy Award. Despite the buzz about the startling statistics, what intrigues us most is the man himself. In the movie we see a side of Gore not seen before—"funny, engaging, open, and downright on fire about getting the surprisingly stirring truth about what he calls our planetary emergency out to ordinary citizens before it's too late."[2] In the fall of 2007 Gore was awarded the Nobel Peace Prize for his important work.

Gore has stepped into his strengths and appears to be his "true" self—a persona all but obliterated during his tenure as vice president and throughout his 2004 presidential campaign. His delivery is compelling and engaging. He has melded his passion for the environment with his strengths of logic and connection to create a stir and, perhaps ultimately, a profound affect in the world.

We cheer him for stepping forth and letting his passion and strengths shine as he plays for high stakes. He has created a "showdown" by turning his best cards face-up and face-out to the world.

High Beams

Once we know our strengths, any fuzziness about our careers and professional goals diminishes considerably, and decisions become easier and straightforward. It's as though we turned on the high beams to illuminate the road and suddenly we see the lane markers much more clearly. Knowledge of our strengths affects our motivation, inspiration, development, and personal sense of satisfaction and fulfillment. Playing to our strengths allows us to design our careers with clarity and purpose, because we are gaining insights to make choices that serve us.

In this chapter, you'll apply your strengths and build them so that they serve you when you need them most. Poker champions in the World Series of Poker bring their best skills to the game to vie for a prize pool. Though you may not be "playing" at work for those kinds of stakes, you probably do want to be as productive and successful as possible.

Narrow Your Focus and Expand Your Sight

While a broad view of our strengths offers us the ability to see an outline of our successes, a narrow focus on strengths reveals the rich, detailed, and complex possibilities to apply them. A simple lesson in backyard astronomy illustrates this concept. When we peer into the night sky, many of the stars we see are part of our own galaxy, the Milky Way, but we also see stars far beyond our galaxy. If we're fortunate enough to be in a place where a clear, dark sky is truly visible, it can reveal a handful of nearby galaxies, each on the fringe of naked-eye visibility. The most obvious and celebrated is the Andromeda Galaxy, 2.5 million light-years away.

How do we actually see Andromeda? We need a strong telescope to focus on a small bit of the sky where Andromeda can be found, magnify it many times, and bring it into more detailed view. What we first saw with the naked eye as a small, blurry image, begins to reveal marvelous complexity, variety, and a myriad of individual stars. When our telescope points at Andromeda, it blocks out distractions—the moon, the Big Dipper, and other stars. Similarly, when we focus on and magnify our strengths, we block out distractions—assumptions about our skills, history, and weaknesses that can overshadow our strengths.

Try this exercise to narrow your focus onto your strengths: Write or draw your strengths in a circle in the center of a blank piece of paper. Use whatever words or images best capture them for you. Around those strengths, brainstorm jobs, roles, industries, careers, activities, volunteer opportunities, recreation possibilities, passions, and interests that leverage one or more of those strengths. Notice how fast the list grows. Stick with it for a while longer, and then ask a creative colleague or friend to add to it. Your list of possibilities is huge, isn't it?

When we focus to skills and experiences, our options contract. When we narrow our focus on our strengths, our options expand. The strength of creativity is useful in a corporate project manager role as well as in a position as artistic director for the local museum. Talent in developing the potential of others applies in a grade school, as a vice president, and when volunteering with an organization such as Big Brother.

Bob, a bored accountant with a strength in analysis, discovered he can work in many functions and doesn't have to rely on his accounting skills. When his focus was limited to his skills, he was unable to see other options. With a broader view that incorporates his strengths, Bob is now considering a wide range of career possibilities that include financial planner, quality assurance agent, and compliance officer. Maria discovered, if she used her strength of visioning (seeing possibilities and paths leading toward them), she could successfully open her own business. When Maria considered only her experience and skills in office management, this possibility never occurred to her. Nancy, despite a lack of experience in the nonprofit sector, realized that the same strengths that made her a competent director of marketing also allowed her to be a savvy executive director for a local, expanding service organization.

Leaving one's current role is by no means the only choice, though. Countless leaders in organizations around the globe have created more opportunities to apply strengths, such as influencing, creativity, communication, humor, putting people at ease, and analysis to their current roles. We propose three ways you can emulate their successes:

1. *Apply* your strengths to your current role;
2. *Adapt* your role to require frequent use of your strengths.
3. *Build* your strengths.

1. Apply Strengths in Your Current Role

To begin playing to your strengths, play close to home. Consider your major tasks, accountabilities, responsibilities, and your unique array of strengths in searching for opportunities to apply your strengths to your current role. Ask yourself:

- ♠ How can my unique strengths serve my work and make me more effective?
- ♠ How well does my current role align with my strengths?
- ♠ Which strengths do I feel compelled to use?
- ♠ Which strengths am I unwilling to postpone using?
- ♠ Which strengths do I want to develop more fully?
- ♠ Which strengths define my leadership style?
- ♠ How can my strengths make all my work more fun, inspiring, and sustaining?
- ♠ How can I build and enhance each strength so I'm even better at it?
- ♠ How can I create more opportunities to use my strengths in my current role?
- ♠ What else is possible if I consciously and intentionally apply my strengths?

Do you feel a sense of power and excitement in your answers? Why wait to apply your strengths? Set yourself up now for success by applying those strengths in as many ways as you can every single day.

Many of your current responsibilities may already align with your strengths. This is great news! Current responsibilities are the perfect "laboratory" in which to focus your attention and practice applying your strengths. Shift how you *view* your current responsibilities, and seek ways to apply your strengths. This enhanced perspective will produce significant new opportunities for you to use your strengths. When you look closely at the possibilities for applying your strengths, and intentionally and passionately do so, you will experience remarkable outcomes.

Build confidence in your strengths by seeking out small opportunities, and use them in new and fresh ways. Apply your strengths as you lead, in meetings you attend, projects you manage, decisions you make, and when coaching others.

Becoming a leader is synonymous with becoming yourself. It is precisely that simple, and it's also that difficult.... First and foremost, find out what it is you're about, and be that.
—*Warren Bennis*

Examine your job tasks and ask yourself *how*—not *if*—you can apply your strengths more fully to that task. And be sure to apply your strengths—your leadership brand—to all aspects of leading.

At B2B Printers, Michael noted that he already uses his strengths of influencing and developing others, and he wondered how he could leverage them further. As a sales professional, Michael applies his influence strength when he closes a deal. To build on that strength, he began to teach the art of closing a deal to account managers, enhancing their skills and increasing their sales. He expanded his influencing strength, used his talent of amplifying to fine-tune processes, and coached and inspired his staff. Each of these strengths works in unison as he builds momentum toward a new vision for his organization.

Be like Mike! We predict you'll feel a surge of enthusiasm for the tasks you've been performing. You'll gain new perspectives and new insights. Best of all, you'll enjoy the fun of being more successful, and success will come with greater ease and pleasure!

Sustain Your Strengths

Consciously playing to your strengths may be a new behavior for you (and probably for your organization), so you may want to pay particular attention to how you sustain focus on your strengths. It's a great idea to bring your manager on board.

Position the conversation with your manager like this: "I want to talk to you about how I can make a greater contribution. I've been learning about what activities play to my strengths, and I think it's possible I can maximize my work to really use my strengths." Ask your manager to think through the strengths she observes in you.

Begin your discussion by sharing your conclusions about your core strengths, and invite your manager to add her observations. Discuss how you might apply those strengths more fully to your current role. Explain your ideas about how you can specifically leverage each strength, and ask for ideas and thoughts about other opportunities to use your strengths more fully. Then, initiate steps toward implementing your strengths, and continue to seek feedback and support.

Another way to sustain your strengths is networking with other leaders, both inside and outside the organization, particularly those who have been discovering and playing to their strengths. Talk about strengths in social situations; if you ask others about *their* strengths, chances are the interaction will generate new ways for everyone to use their strengths.

Most importantly, build a support structure for incorporating your strengths into your work and personal life. Engage a few people in your life to help keep you focused on your strengths and help you identify opportunities to use them. Invite staff members to join your support team—they can provide feedback that clearly indicates what impact you're having when applying your strengths, and where you may be misusing a strength. Engage your spouse or a friend in this dialogue. Remember the strengths-based life is new to most of us. You'll find it much more sustainable if you aren't the only person in your inner circle extolling the virtues of playing to your strengths.

2. ADAPT YOUR ROLE

If you find your current role does *not* allow you to make the most effective use of your strengths, every day, and as often as possible, create opportunities to change it. You can adapt it, mold it, add to it, or subtract from it in creative ways that mirror your strengths.

We're not saying this is easy; you may have to shift some work to someone else. Additionally, you may want to add some new responsibilities to your current role. Therefore, when changing your role, you may have to negotiate with your boss, employees, customers, and peers. They may all be affected by your desired changes. Rest assured, it's worth the extra effort to align your strengths more completely, because the end result will be a wider venue to apply your strengths. It's also a good "practice run" for learning how to develop the strengths of others.

David R. Hawkins argues that, "genius is the capacity for an extraordinary degree of mastery in one's calling." His advice is to "do what you like to do best, and do it to the very best of your ability."[3] Understanding our strengths and choosing to leverage them fully makes us the *real* geniuses of the world.

The first step in the process of adapting your role is one you've already completed—to take as many weaknesses as possible off your plate. When you delegate, purchase, or ignore your weakness, you create space to add much more enticing and "juicy" work! If you haven't finished the work from Chapter 3♠—identifying your weaknesses and moving them off your plate—now is a great time to do so, because you'll need the space for new strength-based work!

*Do what you like to do best, and do it to
the very best of your ability.*
—*David Hawkings*

Revisit your responsibilities, accountabilities, and tasks. Which of these create a feeling of dread, inadequacy, or low energy?

It's likely those tasks are weaknesses, best handled by delegating, purchasing, or ignoring. We invite you now to take a second look at your list, mining for those activities that don't seem to align with your strengths in any inspiring way. For example, sending invoices is a task that makes little use of Carol's core strengths. However, it isn't a weakness. She has the analytical and detail capability to do the task well. She considered purchasing the skill set, but wasn't motivated to do that because the task is actually easy for her. So instead, she allocates one hour on the last day of the month for invoicing. It is concise; she created a tight and manageable process, and she completes it quickly and easily. This is one of the strategies for managing an activity that does not capitalize on your strengths, and yet can't be dismissed altogether: you allocate a specified amount of time to complete the activity each day, week, or month.

Which of your responsibilities really do not—and seemingly cannot—capitalize on your strengths? Perhaps you can alter or change some of the activities that don't make full use of your strengths.

If your strength is to improve existing ideas, ask your staff to present at least one solution to a problem they bring to you—even if the solution is silly or impractical. If ideas fascinate you,

you see connections between seemingly unrelated things; if you're a little bored once a solution surfaces, insert yourself sooner into problem-resolution processes. Then leave the implementation to someone else.

> ♠
> *If we don't change direction soon,*
> *we'll end up where we're going.*
> *—Irwin Corey*
> ♠

Be brutally honest when you answer this question: What do I really want to let go of because it does not align with my strengths? For now, ignore the barriers. Allegedly practical and rational thinking may set limits or suggest what you can't do. You might find excuses popping into your head, such as, "I can't—my boss would never let me!" or, "That's essential to my role—if I let it go, I know I'll be doomed." This "gremlin" voice is giving you some useful information—to remove these activities may require some renegotiation with your boss, staff, or customers! Don't let this stop you from persisting in taking these activities off your plate.

Eliminating responsibilities is one way of adapting your role to maximize your strengths. Adding responsibilities is another. You probably have many great ideas to maximize your unique pattern of strengths, such as:

- ♠ Adding a new project.
- ♠ Volunteering for a task force.
- ♠ Offering to do a presentation for your boss.
- ♠ Analyzing the department statistics.
- ♠ Developing a class to teach others.

♠ Partnering with a colleague to take on more of *her* areas of nonstrength while giving her some of *yours*.

♠ Forming a team to do some research.

♠ Creating a scorecard for your department.

♠ Helping a colleague create his implementation plan.

♠ Designing a new customer awareness campaign.

♠ Offering to mentor a coworker.

Other useful activities to incorporate your strengths into your current or newly changed role include:

♠ Creating a list of your strengths and post it where you, family, and coworkers will see it.

♠ Adding your strengths and/or your leadership brand to your e-mail signature line. This invites others to ask about your strengths, to come to you for your wisdom, and to identify situations in their lives that call for your strengths.

♠ Adding a column to your to-do list that identifies the strength(s) you intend to apply to each task or accountability.

♠ Starting a discussion group with other leaders regarding what they're learning about their strengths.

♠ Hiring a coach. We happen to know a few excellent leadership coaches, but you may have one of your own. Invite your coach to challenge you to build and apply your strengths.

♠ Write your personal mission or purpose statement and, with power and intention, using your strengths to achieve it. You'll find an exercise to create a purpose statement on our Website.

3. BUILD YOUR STRENGTHS

When we ask coaching clients how they will build competence in their strengths, they initially draw a blank. "Build competence or capability in my *strength*?" That's something few of us ever think about. Yet, this is a great opportunity not only to play *to* your strengths, but also to play *with* them.

♠

Your purpose is anything that touches your heart and makes a difference to you.
—*Marcia Wieder*

♠

James Woods is among the growing sector of celebrities bit by the "poker bug." Intrigued by the mental and emotional challenges of poker, Woods actively and energetically pursues advice and lessons from professionals who precede him. He is "a humble student of the game. He is a poker sponge, actively soaking up poker information via every available resource. He reads about poker, talks about poker, watches poker greats playing, plays against poker greats, and is steadily working to become an ambassador of poker."[4] The more Woods builds on his talent for poker, the more his strength increases.

People with artistic strengths often love to learn new media; those with musical strengths often learn to play a wide range of instruments even though they may specialize in one. If you have an athletic strength, wouldn't it be great fun if we asked you to set aside one day a week for golf lessons to build your strength of hand-eye coordination? That's what building your strengths is all about. There's much joy in it!

For today's leaders, many important strengths are intellectual or relationship-based. Seeing the big picture, making connections among disparate ideas, or discovering root causes are examples of intellectual strengths. We may also possess strengths in influencing, creating intimate and trusting relationships, or in empathy. These are relationship-based strengths. Similar to strengths in athletics or the arts, intellectual, relationship, and accomplishment-based strengths can be nurtured and expanded, growing their effectiveness.

While Michael, of B2B Printers, noted that he already initiates, influences, amplifies, and develops others in his role, he discounted his strength of learning. He hadn't realized the contribution he could make by applying it. As Michael reconsidered his responsibilities in light of his natural talent for learning, he allowed himself to look "outside the box" of his company's processes. He conducted research to learn about sales process advancements in other industries and applied lessons learned to make more effective use of his sales team.

Often, we are so comfortable in our strengths that we don't have the language, models, or steps to express how we "do" them. Opening ourselves to learn more about a strength provides us with a language—a lexicon—that enables us to better explain and teach them to others. It also allows us to isolate its various components. Right now, we may use this strength so quickly and intuitively that we don't know how to break it down into its components. Once we understand the components, we can tweak and exercise them, and watch as they become stronger.

Imagine you decide to take a course in classical music appreciation. You recognize the "1812 Overture" because you heard it in the Quaker Oats commercials on television, but that's about the extent of your knowledge. When your instructor first introduces you to Tchaikovsky's "Nutcracker Suite," you experience the power of the piece as a whole. You hear all the instruments together, creating a beautiful, orchestrated sound. With training, however, you begin to differentiate the violins from the oboes. You begin to hear how the different sections contribute to the work.

You will be most optimistic, most coura-geous, and most ambitious when playing to an area of strength.
—Marcus Buckingham

You feel how the conductor builds the volume of the strings or softens the percussion to create a certain emotion, mood, or expression. That's what you can achieve with increased knowledge about your strengths. You "hear" them better, and learn to play them like a fine symphony.

We like the way Marcus Buckingham writes about the power of growing your strengths:

> You may not be creative in all aspects of your life, but whatever your general level of creativity may be, you will

> be at the peak of your creative powers in your areas of strength. You may not be a naturally inquisitive person, but you will be at your most inquisitive in your areas of strength. You will be most optimistic, most courageous, and most ambitious when playing to an area of strength. And when you hit resistance or obstacles to your goals, you will bounce back fastest when those goals center on one of your strengths…you will learn the most, grow the most, and develop the most in your areas of greatest strength. Your strengths are your multiplier. Your strengths magnify you.[5]

To deepen your insights into your strengths, consider:

♠ Who can I talk to, to learn more about this strength? For example, a senior leader who demonstrates a strategic strength might teach you more about how to take your strategic thoughts and put them into action. Or, you notice the chair of your neighborhood association seems to share your natural strength of facilitating others to reach consensus. What can you learn from her effectiveness?

♠ What might I read to expand my competence in this strength? People with a strength in taking command of situations often like to read military histories to learn about successful strategies. While they may have a natural repertoire of their own methods, they find what others do with their strategic talent to be fascinating. Those who influence others easily might find it intriguing to look at the precise steps used by Dale Carnegie in his forever popular book, *How to Win Friends and Influence People* (Simon & Schuster Inc., 1998).

♠ What tools can I use to learn more about this strength? For example, leaders who excel in analysis might learn about software systems or process improvement models to put more structures around their analysis, giving themselves an improved language to understand and communicate their strength.

♠ Who will I partner with to complement my strength? Leaders strong in creating vision often partner with someone strong in identifying action steps. Both parties expand the capacity of their strengths in this manner.

♠ How do I apply my strengths outside work? We can serve others, gain personal satisfaction, and extend our strengths by applying them to church activities, volunteer and community service projects, and by helping friends, family, and neighbors. This increases our personal satisfaction outside work while building experience in using our strengths, ultimately assisting us in applying them more effectively and powerfully back at work.

Bumblebees

Years ago, scientists researched the flight patterns of bumblebees and houseflies. They put groups of each insect in narrow-mouthed bottles and observed if and how they escaped.

Insanity: doing the same thing over and over again and expecting different results.
—Variously attributed to Albert Einstein and Rita Mae Brown

After the first week, the bees lay dead in the bottom of their bottle, but the flies buzzed around the laboratory. Upon closer scrutiny, the scientists noticed that the bees flew directly into the glass at roughly the same place, in the same direction, time after time. After hundreds of contacts with the side of the bottle, exhausted and beaten, they fell to the bottom and died. The flies, however, escaped from the bottle. Why? Because they continually experimented—

hitting the side in one place, then redirecting higher, lower, or to the other side with each new attempt. They finally zeroed in on the opening and escaped! Their headache was a small price for freedom.

Similar to the bumblebees, we often go about activities mindlessly in the same way, pursuing the same types of learning opportunities year after year. Instead, choose to have fun! As kids, we learned through play. Anyone who hangs around kids knows that the *work* of a child is *play*. What a great way to learn! Why have we forgotten this lesson as adults? Having fun while learning is something kids have all over us. They may not know they're learning, but we know they'll always learn better if it's fun. Making mistakes and laughing at yourself is an integral part of fun. When the ocean wave throws us off our boogie board, or we tumble down a snowy slope on new skis, we laugh, even as we rub the sore places. Try on a new, strengths-based behavior one day and see what happens. Play with your strengths! Let your inner kid out!

Is a New Job Required?

We've looked at how to apply your strengths to your current role, how you can adapt your role to create more opportunities to use your strengths, how you might build your strengths to be more competent and clear, and how to sustain these changes.

Clearly, strengths will make our current responsibilities more exciting and engaging! However, if the examination of possibilities to use strengths in your current role leads you to believe that opportunities are sorely lacking, or if you feel "stuck" in your current role, it may be worthwhile to consider alternative venues for playing to your strengths. Simply put, it may be time to look for a new job— one that fits your strengths.

Remember Terry from Chapter 2♠, the coaching client who never seemed to be able to please his boss? As director of training and

Never continue a job you don't enjoy. If you're happy in what you're doing, you'll like yourself, you'll have inner peace. And if you have that, along with physical health, you will have had more success than you could possibly have imagined.
—Johnny Carson

development for a high technology company, Terry excelled. Yet, his core strengths of creativity, developing others, and forming strategy were not valued in his organization. During Andrea's coaching work with him, Terry saw how using these strengths at work would lead to more joy, fulfillment, and success. Terry left that organization and moved on to a highly successful career in an organization in which he plays to his strengths.

Terry assessed his role and his organization clearly, and made the tough decision to move on. Some of you reading this may feel the same pull, and, you may feel stuck right now. Corporate roles can seduce us into believing we would be sacrificing pay, job security, tenure, and/or our reputation if we left to go to another organization. But you aren't stuck! Your strengths bolster your confidence when those "golden handcuffs" feel like ties that bind. You don't have to stay in that job, work for the organization you now work for, or live in the same neighborhood. You can make major changes in your life because knowledge of your strengths serves as a strong foundation for change in the right direction, for the right reasons. You can use your strengths to create an exit strategy as well as to design your new role, career, or life change. And you can ensure that you will have lots of opportunity to do what you do best every single day if you keep your strengths at the forefront of your job/career search.

We have clients who finally decide that their strengths of autonomy, independence, and taking full ownership of their lives compel them to start their own businesses. (We've experienced this urge ourselves!) This is a viable alternative, if the decision aligns with your strengths. We have other clients who shift inside their own organizations, because they feel like they've used up their creativity and ability to formulate strategy in a position they've held for a long time. Our client, Steve, took a lateral move in his organization, for just that reason. He enjoyed a surge of creativity when he applied his strengths to new responsibilities. We've worked with leaders who have abandoned their industries altogether because other lines of work called for more of their innate strengths. When these moves are aligned with strengths—and not simply driven by politics or an opportunity for a higher salary or a shorter commute—the results can be powerful.

A Crucial Overlap

Looking at strengths objectively guides us in these important career and personal decisions. When we combine our strengths with our passions, and seek options that will sustain us financially, we dramatically increase our chances for success. The crucial overlap, as illustrated in the following model on the next page, is where passion, strength, and financial viability come together in that perfect career opportunity.

Unfortunately, especially when we've experienced a good-paying job, we make our decisions based more on what we perceive will sustain us financially, and underrate the importance of our passions and strengths. Including your passions and strengths as you seek a new way to contribute will drive even greater success. A mentor once offered this sage advice: "Figure out what you really love to do, and then find someone who will pay you for doing it."

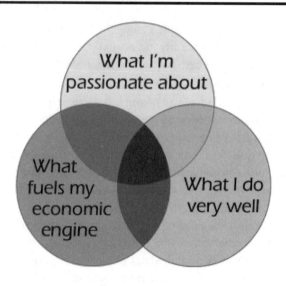

We suspect that, if you are thinking about changing jobs, some key questions are already in your mind, such as, "Do I have the financial resources to make this happen? Do I have the support? Is this a wise career move?" We want to suggest some additional questions that are important, but may not be among the first ones you've considered:

- ♠ What do I feel when I fully engage my strengths? What would it feel like to do that more often?

- ♠ What have I done well in the past, but no longer have the opportunity to do?

- ♠ What contribution do I feel compelled to make that cannot occur in my current role/organization?

- ♠ What's intriguing, exciting, and perhaps scary about making that contribution happen?

♠ How will my strengths support me in the transition itself?

♠ What resources do I need to bolster these strengths?

♠ Who can I partner with to help me make the best decisions?

Showdown—Playing for High Stakes

Gallup's research shows that only one in five workers plays to her strengths every day. Did you also know that the *higher* an employee climbs in an organization, the *less* likely it is that he uses his strengths every day?[6] Isn't that sad? We wonder why that happens. Why have we designed our organizations so that the *more* a person progresses in her career, the *less* likely she is to use her strengths? Or do employees feel so compelled to continue to climb the career ladder that they unwittingly collude in using fewer and fewer of their strengths, in exchange for greater salary, influence, and perceived job security? Either way, the tragedy is that our emerging leaders are shaping and maintaining organizational cultures that will only make it harder for them and others to perform at their best.

Now that you know your strengths, you can buck that trend.

Leaders who consciously and intentionally incorporate strengths into their work open the possibility for stellar performance and spectacular results. By playing their strongest cards, they are more successful and attract more opportunities to repeat those successes.

Implementation Ideas

APPLY YOUR STRENGTHS IN YOUR CURRENT ROLE

Remember your leadership brand, think hard about your current role, and answer these questions:

- ♠ How can my unique strengths serve my work and make me more effective?
- ♠ How well does my current role align with my strengths?
- ♠ Which strengths do I feel compelled to use?
- ♠ Which strengths am I unwilling to postpone using?
- ♠ Which strengths do I want to develop more fully?
- ♠ Which strengths define my leadership style?
- ♠ How can my strengths make all my work more fun, inspiring, and sustaining?
- ♠ How can I build and enhance each strength so I'm even better at it?
- ♠ How can I create more opportunities to use my strengths in my current role?
- ♠ What else is possible if I consciously and intentionally apply my strengths?

Based on your answers to the questions, set some goals for yourself, and identify tasks or steps you'll take toward achieving them. Include these in the "Apply Strengths" column in the following Strengths Development Plan. (Download a blank version of this form on our Website at *www.play2yourstrengths.com*.)

Strength	Apply Strengths: What opportunities do I have now to use my strengths more?	Adapt Roles: What opportunities can I create to use strengths more?	Build Strengths: How can I improve my strengths?	Take Specific Actions: Set SMART goals
1. Creativity (Example)	-Finance project -Development team	-Joint venture w/Bob	-Take an art class -Add stories to presentations	-Resolve JV idea w/ Bob by 5:30
2.				
3.				
4.				

ADAPT YOUR ROLE

Change your current role, adding and eliminating specific responsibilities so that you can apply your strengths more every day. In your Strengths Development Plan, complete the column labeled "Adapt Role."

BUILD YOUR STRENGTHS

Look for inspiring and creative ways to build your strengths: reading, taking a class, establishing a partnership, applying your strengths in volunteer or family activities. Challenge yourself to apply, teach, and incorporate the value and contribution of your unique strengths. Add your ideas to the "Build Strengths" column in your Strengths Development Plan.

Sustain Your Strengths

Set up structures that will support you—friends, colleagues, staff members, peers—or hire a leadership coach. Engage your manager in the changes you wish to make. If you decide to leave the organization, your support structure needs to be even stronger. Get help to ensure you stay on track with your goals and aspirations.

Claim Your Purpose

Write a purpose statement. Knowing your purpose will guide your decisions and reveal opportunities to leverage your strengths. (There's guidance on how to create your purpose statement on our Website.)

Practice Mind-Mapping

To learn about mind mapping—the tool you used to identify your strengths in a circle and brainstorm options for their use—pick up *The Mind Map Book: How to Use Radiant Thinking to Maximize Your Brain's Untapped Potential* by Tony Buzan and Barry Buzan (Plume, 1996).

Read an Article on Leadership and Strengths

Read Robert E. Quinn's July–August 2005 *Harvard Business Review* article, "Moments of Greatness: Entering the Fundamental State of Leadership," pages 77 to 83.

There is another great article in the February 2007 *Harvard Business Review,* "In Praise of the Incomplete Leader" by Deborah Ancona, Thomas W. Malone, Wanda J. Orlikowski, and Peter M. Senge, pages 92 to 100. The overview paragraph reads, "No leader is perfect. The best ones don't try to be—they concentrate on honing their strengths and find others who can make up for their limitations."

CHAPTER FIVE

ANTE UP:

BUILDING THE KITTY

Ante is the money placed in the pot before a hand begins.
Ante up: To put one's ante in the pot.

Have you ever hired someone with excellent experience, who interviewed great, only to discover later that he was missing a critical strength? Changing your management processes to cultivate strengths will make your staff richer and your winnings bigger. It's understandable if you're wincing, because change can be challenging. Yet, change is necessary if you wish to reap the benefits of a strengths-based focus. Lee Garcia, occasional writer for Poker Player online, characterizes it like this:

> When a pitcher is giving up runs, he changes his style. If they're hitting his fastball, he'll throw sliders. If they're slamming the curveballs, he'll throw fastballs. A poker player needs to do the same thing. If they know how you are playing and can get a decent read on you, you have to change up just like the pitcher. The point is that you can't just sit there and wallow in misery; you have to change something! Get out of your favorite seat

or game and try something different. Every time you change something, it's a new beginning. Look at it as a fresh start...it can only get better.[1]

In this chapter we explore how strengths can improve the basic management processes you use every day: hiring, managing performance, delegating, accountability, rewarding, and developing your people. Creating strengths-based management processes requires a bigger investment and more thought up front. You'll have to "ante up" a bit more. However, cultivating strengths in your staff makes your management job easier, and wins you a larger pot!

Having a clear picture of both the strengths your team *possesses* and those that are *missing* helps you acquire, retain, and inspire great talent, so you can achieve your most important goals. Shift your critical people-management processes to enrich the conversations you will soon have with each of your staff members about his strengths.

Red Ink

It's no wonder we focus on our weaknesses—we learned all about them in school. Remember when you studied hard for your English test? You worked through the questions feeling confident in your knowledge, and then experienced that terrible day when your test came back and looked like the teacher had bled all over it. She highlighted where you misspelled a word, or had odd sentence structure, or checked the wrong answer. The more red you saw, the more your hopes sank. You didn't need to look at the teacher's comments; you simply eyeballed the quantity of red and knew how poorly you'd done.

Back then, and even still today, teachers, more often than not, highlighted what you did wrong. Even if you received a passing grade, you probably examined the red marks first. What did I do wrong? Where was I less than perfect? We know from decades of research in behavioral psychology that learning can occur from both positive and negative reinforcement. All too often, in education and in corporate America, the focus is on the negative—the mistakes and failures. Wouldn't learning be more productive, motivational, and fun if there was a focus on the positive—your strengths and successes? Remember how discouraging that focus on mistakes, errors, failures, and weaknesses was? Did the red ink make you feel proud, accomplished, and good about yourself? Hardly. Did it make you feel like you were never quite good enough? Perhaps. Undoubtedly, focusing on weakness makes us feel physically drained, emotionally wrung out, disheartened, frustrated, and defeated.

More important, how clear were you, after reading your teacher's red remarks, about what you did *well*? Could you see your strengths in the comments? You probably learned what not to do, but how much did you learn from the red marks about what to repeat? You only knew this by deduction. You may have thought, "If I take away the places where I messed up, what remains are the places where I did okay, right?" But that begs the next questions: Where did I excel? What did I do really well, so I can be more successful the next time? That valuable information simply does not exist in the red-ink feedback process. As a result, you were denied a great learning opportunity to know more about your strengths—and how to make them better, to build on them, and to apply them for success the next time. You wanted to say, "Tell me what I did well, so I can do it again!"

How many managers at your work operate using the "red-ink" approach? If there is feedback at all, more likely than not, it is of the red-ink variety. Deadlines, high expectations, the quick pace at the office, stress and pressure, or lack of confidence and skill can lead us to focus our attention on what went wrong. In our meetings, we talk about why customer satisfaction dropped from 98 to 96 percent, without paying a lot of attention to why we hit 96! On Monday mornings when teams get together for a 15-minute status meeting—some are even held standing up to keep them short and fast— what's the focus? What did we do well last week? What successes did we enjoy? What behaviors should we repeat? Hardly ever! We focus on what went wrong and what we're doing to fix it. Our individual one-on-one meetings with staff members can fall into the same trap—discussing where the employee didn't perform up to par, his weaknesses, the opportunities for improvement. It's not too hard for an employee, and the entire staff, to feel a little (or a lot) depressed in this scenario. There's a palpable sense of no one ever being quite good enough.

Don't get us wrong...particularly when the stakes are high, mistakes can be costly. It's simply that the "squeaky wheel" (a mistake or error) gets the grease—and we continue to grease that wheel over and over, often neglecting to notice how well the other wheels are functioning.

Tom Rath, author of *StrengthsFinder 2.0*, talks about the results of a survey conducted by Gallup that examined what happens when your manager ignores you, focuses on your strengths, or focuses on your weaknesses. The data revealed some startling facts:

- ♠ If your manager *ignores* you, you have a 40-percent chance of being actively disengaged in your work.

- ♠ If your manager focuses on your *weaknesses*, you have a 22-percent chance of being actively disengaged.

- ♠ If your manager focuses on your *strengths*, you have a mere 1-percent chance of being actively disengaged.

We found that if your manager focuses on your strengths, your chances of being actively disengaged go down to one in 100.
—*Tom Rath*

Clearly, being ignored is the worst possible state. Attention, even to our weaknesses, is better than no attention at all. But for 99 percent of your team to be engaged, a focus on strengths is a huge lever!

Rath goes on to talk about how a negative person—the team member who drags everyone else down—can shift away from negativity when his manager focuses on his strengths.

Focusing on strengths as part of the team's foundation creates significant team alignment. Team members are incited to collaborate effectively rather than compete with each other, creating a synergy that ultimately enhances outcomes through each member's strength. Marcus Buckingham calls strengths the "master lever." "Pull this lever and an engaged and productive team will be the result. Fail to pull it and no matter what else is done to motivate the team, it'll never fully engage. It will never become a high performance team…You don't focus on people's strength to make them happier. You do it to make them better performers."[2] Actually, focusing on strengths accomplishes both.

What we pay attention to is what we reinforce. How different it is when managers pay attention to what went right! When we illuminate what created success, we start seeing and reinforcing strengths. We notice that Howard did a great job yesterday, inspiring the team when the system crashed. We didn't even know Howard could do that! How can we put him in a position to do more of that? We saw Karen figuring out important work for us to do while the system was down. She does that, have you noticed? She always seems to know what the priorities are. Marco quickly came up with a temporary, viable solution to the problem that allowed us to keep the system semi-functional while others on the team worked on the bigger fix. Brilliant! Timely! Collaborative! Positive!

We encourage you to shift the lens through which you manage people, from "what went wrong" to "what went right" Management guru Ken Blanchard's adage, "Catch them doing it right!" is great advice. Focus yourself and your staff on how to apply strengths to forward the goals of the department, and you will boost employee engagement and productivity.

123

The Processes of People Management

In this chapter, we're looking at the *processes* of managing your people, not so much the specific strengths innate to each of your employees. If you're eager to find out how to help your employees identify and apply their strengths, flip forward to Chapter 6♠. But if you're willing, we thought we'd invite you to look at your basic people-management processes first, to see how these processes can improve through strengths.

Brian Brim, in his article for the *Gallup Management Journal*, writes about the developing familiarity executives and managers have with the "strengths-based approach" to leading. "When organizations take a strengths-based approach to managing their employees—when they hire, develop, and deploy people in ways that help them maximize their innate talents—their employees can make powerful, positive contributions to driving the business forward."

This is your chance to lead from your own strengths as you begin to talk about and model your strengths in service to others.

Hiring is a great process to begin shifting toward strengths, because you already know the sage advice about hiring—hire people more competent than you. Sometimes, this can be challenging—it can be hard to find the right competence at the right time. Further, our egos might get in the way when we face a hiring decision. However, if we hire people more competent than we are, we have an easier job leading them, and we create greater excellence in our people and our departments.

When managers have job openings or valuable "headcounts," they examine the skills currently in their work groups, identify missing skills, and hire to fill the gaps. Perhaps an administrative person is what we need right now. Maybe we need someone who understands the quality process, or who is up-to-date on a critical piece of software. This is a good thing! What possibilities open up if we also look at our existing group—and an opportunity to hire someone new—from the perspective of strengths? Remember that strengths are innate gifts or talents, while knowledge and skills are acquired.

We can acquire knowledge and learn skills, but we need to hire for innate strengths.

Hiring

When our hero, Michael (the sales director at B2B Printers), examined his team through his newfound lens of strengths, he discovered strength in the areas of influencing and achieving. These are typical strengths of sales leaders, don't you think? They tend to be likeable and engaging, and they are motivated and inspired—even driven—by their innate talent for achievement. They know how to pace themselves and how to realize achievement, bit by bit, customer by customer, sale by sale.

One of the key strengths missing from Michael's team was analysis—the ability to see patterns and connections in numbers and data, and to enjoy looking for these patterns. Also in short supply was the visioning strength—the ability to see possibilities and the paths toward them. Both of these strengths would round out Michael's staff.

So, when Michael had an opening for a new sales associate, for what did he search? Instead of bringing on board yet another sales person who was highly effective at managing relationships, he sought a person who was intrigued by and highly competent at working with numbers, analyzing figures, and gathering data to project the future. Instead of looking for 10 years sales experience (comprised of skills and knowledge), he became more interested in finding the *strengths* to complement his group. If he found a candidate with a true strength and passion for analysis and strategy, it would matter little how much sales experience she possessed. As a matter of fact, if she had been applying this strength in a nonsales environment, her strength might add even more knowledge into the mix!

Michael took a strengths-based approach to this job opening. He posted the role with different language instead of using the same job description from the last three hires. He looked at the candidates through a different lens. He sought a person who would not simply perform, the analysis and strategic projections, but who was actually excited to do so—because he had an inherent strength and passion for it. He eventually hired Anna, who had a sales background in retail, a very different industry, but who appeared to have just the strengths Michael sought—analysis and strategy. We'll revisit Anna a little later in this chapter.

The Right Player
With the Right Strengths
in the Right Position

In the world of baseball, few have affected the game as much as Yogi Berra. Today, Yogi is well-known for his interesting statements, a strength used as a player, coach, and manager, often to get attention. Yogi became baseball's irreverent spokesman. As a world-class catcher, Yogi directed his teammates with exceptional understanding of the game, the players' strengths, the strategic situation, and the opponents. As a manager, he used the same understanding of men and baseball, and made his mark. Yogi retired from baseball in 1989 after making the most of his strengths throughout his career. And with his infamous wit, he made our world a more colorful place. A few of the interesting comments attributed to Yogi are:

- ♠ "I really didn't say everything that I said."
- ♠ "If you don't know where you're going you'll go somewhere else."
- ♠ "It's like déjà vu all over again."
- ♠ "It ain't over 'til it's over."
- ♠ "You can observe a lot by watching."
- ♠ "Think? How the hell are you going to think and hit at the same time?"

Imagining Yogi in a corporate setting makes us laugh, but he did understand the critical role of a manager to assist others in finding their strengths and making the most of them. Yogi knew that in business or baseball, the right player with the right strengths in the right position is a leadership essential, and is magnificent to watch.

How do you begin to hire for strengths? Once you've identified the strengths you need, you have to be able to assess your candidate's strengths. Unfortunately, because the strengths-based approach is in its infancy in our world of work and school, we don't have much language or experience to ferret out strengths in an interview. We have to learn to probe a little deeper—to look for patterns and themes that underlie the individual's successes and accomplishments.

Our candidates don't help us much, either. Some résumés, these days, list "strengths," but, for the most part, they focus on skills and knowledge; specifically, what the candidate can do, has done, and will do. While skills and knowledge are important to hiring managers, they are insufficient if you want a perfect hire. Instead, look for underlying strengths that are applicable across a wide range of opportunities and skills.

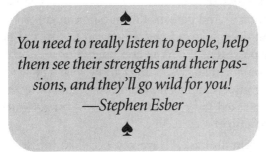

♠

You need to really listen to people, help them see their strengths and their passions, and they'll go wild for you!
—Stephen Esber

♠

Asking candidates about their strengths is one way to begin. In a recent interview, our friend, Rich, listed these as his strengths:

127

- ♠ Oration.
- ♠ Empathy.
- ♠ Organizing/prioritizing.
- ♠ High computer literacy.

Now, savvy readers, which of these are strengths and which are skills? Oration is a skill, as is computer literacy. But what about the others—what about empathy and organizing/prioritizing? While they may not be specific strengths, they give clues to the deeper nature of how Rich sees his capabilities.

A strengths-based manager looking for specific strengths would probe these two answers to see if Rich can identify the underlying inherent talent that is strong in him. Yes, oration might also reflect an underlying strength; however, it may take longer to uncover this information in your interview, because that item is so clearly a skill.

How do you probe this way? A few obvious questions probably came to your mind, such as "Tell, me, Rich—what talent or strength do you possess that underlies the skill of 'organization and prioritization'?" And perhaps this question might work for empathy: "What does the word *empathy* mean to you and how do you know you possess it?" Rich's answer might provide you with insight into his strength. If he says, "I don't know what it is—I seem to have a knack for understanding how someone might be feeling in a situation," you asked the right question and—bingo—identified the strength of empathy!

You might also ask, "Have you ever had to use your skill of organizing to organize other people? Tell me about a time you did that and felt you were successful." Or, for empathy: "Tell me about a situation at work, within the last six months, in which you were challenged to use your strength of empathy." This type of question will help your candidate expound on his strength, and give you good data about its depth. Did he say "empathy" because he thought you wanted to hear it, or did his response indicate a deep knowledge of what empathy is, and how he leverages it when needed?

Self-Employment, Self-Fulfillment?

According to a survey conducted in 2000 by Dartmouth College economist David G. Blanchflower and his colleagues, 71 percent of Americans would prefer working for themselves to working for an employer.[3] It strikes us that this significant figure is potentially a manifestation of the compelling desire for strength-based work among employees themselves. Do workers desire to become self-employed so that they can do more of the things they do not do well? Of course not! Entrepreneur after entrepreneur, corporate escapee after corporate escapee, starts his own business so that he can do exactly what he wants to do: maximize his strengths, excel at his passion, and succeed on his own terms.

Once he opens his business, he targets his work so it absolutely makes the best use of his personal and organizational strengths. By the way, this is what marketing is all about—identifying what you are astoundingly good at as a small-business owner or a self-employed consultant (or job seeker!) and marketing that. It is how entrepreneurs succeed, prosper, and thrive!

We wonder how much the tide of self-employment might be (restoring healthy talent pools to organizations that desperately need employees) if leaders in organizations made excellent use of their employees' strengths so they weren't compelled to go out and create strengths-based work on their own! This intriguing notion deserves more research.

Managing Performance

Back at B2B Printers, four weeks pass and Anna arrives for her first day of work. Michael, continuing his strengths-based management approach, now asks himself, "What does Anna need in order to ensure her rapid and spectacular success in applying her strengths?" Do you see how different this question is than, "What does Anna need to know?" The latter question would lead Michael to pile manuals on Anna's desk, to get her "familiar" with the products of B2B. Seriously boring! How could she keep herself from falling asleep while reading this stuff on her first day? She may even think, "Did I make a mistake leaving my old company?"

Michael and Anna agree that they want to get Anna up to speed with absolutely everything she needs in order to apply her strengths every day—so they begin with a purposeful, specific step. What Anna needs right now is context. She is the expert in analysis and projection, so she needs to know the framework in which she can apply her strengths—and she's champing at the bit to do so! Together, Michael and Anna decide she needs to learn about the market where B2B sells products so she can research the trends in those markets, leading to projections that are more accurate. Michael has the great idea that Anna should attach herself to an order—from the beginning of a customer relationship through contracting for sale, to product delivery, to ongoing customer service—to understand the processes she will soon be analyzing.

Now, Michael is able to set short-term performance measures with Anna that are motivating and targeted toward the outcome he is trying to achieve: excellent analysis and accurate projections. Anna will be able to apply her strengths almost immediately.

Yes, this approach to setting performance goals is customized to every hire, because each person brings a unique web of talents and strengths on which to capitalize. If you have a standard process for orienting the generic "new hire," you may have to throw it away. (And good riddance!) You're leveraging strengths from day one, and that looks different from employee to employee. Remember, you're anteing up—you're building the kitty for a bigger payoff! You're investing in your group's excellent performance.

SMART Goals

In his book, *The Psychology of Winning*, Denis Waitley said, "The reason most people never reach their goals is that they don't define them, or ever seriously consider them as believable or achievable. Winners can tell you where they are going, what they plan to do along the way, and who will be sharing the adventure with them."

Strengths-based managers understand the importance of establishing clear, specific, tangible goals directly linked to employee strengths, to guide and motivate their work efforts. Within a few months of Anna's first day at B2B Printers, her onboarding and orientation complete, we know it's time for her to be clear about Michael's expectations of her, as well as her own expectations, and lock her performance goals and measures into place.

Managers and leaders set direction for others by helping them set clear goals. Goals drive action toward the ultimate desired outcomes and results. Setting performance goals is a process you know well if you manage others. Effective goals must demonstrate a few key characteristics to guide employees to move forward productively—they must be "SMART" goals: Specific, Measurable, Action-oriented, Realistic, and Time-based. "Increase customer satisfaction survey scores by five percent at year-end" is a SMART goal. "Improve customer service" is not.

Specific

Measurable

Action-oriented

Realistic

Time-based

♠ Specific: The goal explicitly describes a clear target.

♠ Measurable: The goal includes tangible measures. Measures help someone know exactly what he is accountable for, how to track progress, and how to determine success.

♠ Action-oriented—The goal calls for immediate, clear action.

♠ Realistic: A SMART goal is both realistic (possible to do) and relevant (the right thing to do). A critical look at how possible it is prevents "pie in the sky" goals. Relevance links the goal to the organization's mission.

♠ Time-based: The goal clearly states when it is to be accomplished.

Setting performance goals and measures isn't very different in a strengths-based approach. The goals should be SMART, and the manager and the employee should agree upon them. The difference is in the focus of the goals. As managers, we are often excited when we make a job offer and it is accepted. We believe we hired the best person or, at least, the best person available today. It's a management "high" when a talented person accepts your offer to come work with you. However, all too soon the honeymoon is over, and suddenly you see everything he doesn't have; what he doesn't know about your products and services; who he doesn't know in the company; the politics, the culture, the processes of which he is unaware. And you want him to get it all dialed in—fast.

In the strengths-based approach, the manager resists trying to fill all the knowledge and skill gaps—all the "holes" in the new hire's competence—all of his weaknesses, for heaven's sake. Instead, as in Anna's case, Michael continued to ask the question: "What does Anna need now to ensure her rapid and spectacular success in applying her strengths?" Perhaps she has created a new approach to analyzing sales data, but now she needs to build relationships that enable her to influence "the powers that be" to consider a new process. Anna has already created some good relationships; she has begun to connect with the right people, gain their respect, and influence them. Great! She appears to have a strength in building relationships. Anna now has an opportunity to build on this strength! All she needs is Michael's help identifying important relationships, and some key introductions to send her on her way.

Michael applied a basic tool of strengths-based development when he asked Anna to articulate the steps she used to build relationships with her peers, Justin and Derek. This helped her clearly see the steps to her success, and inspired her to be thoughtful and deliberate in her approach to forming new relationships. Michael's question had a double impact. First, he helped her see her current strength by highlighting the successful relationships she'd already built, increasing her self-confidence. Further, by examining the steps she used to create successful relationships in the past, Anna also understood what she needed to do as she anticipated building *new* ones. Focusing your people on what worked well for them previously builds confidence and clarity about what may work great for them in the future.

Now, from a solid foundation of understanding Anna's strengths, they set her performance objectives. Setting performance objectives based on her strengths supports Michael's goals and motivates Anna. She is confident, excited, and sees that she can build on her existing strength to become even better at forming important relationships. This also supports her in enhancing her greatest strengths of analyzing and visioning. This is a reinforcing, perpetuating circle! (Positive reinforcement—remember that from Psychology 101?) She is so inspired by the idea of building on her strengths that she signs up for a class on creating excellent relationships, realizing that there may be something she can learn. Everyone wins big!

Michael was successful in setting strength-based objectives with Anna. How can you apply what we learned from Michael? Consider these important questions for each of your employees:

- ♠ What are this employee's strengths?
- ♠ What strengths are needed for his unique role?
- ♠ How well do his strengths match up with his role?

♠ How can we capitalize on his strengths?

♠ How can we alter his job so he can use more of his strengths?

Delegating to Build Strength

We all know there are many good reasons to delegate. You might delegate to take things off your plate and free you up for other priorities. You might delegate to build a staff member's proficiency in a particular skill or knowledge. You might delegate to educate or to assess competence. You might delegate to expand the knowledge, skills, and competence applied to a particular task or problem. There are many excellent reasons to delegate.

As a matter of fact, the good reasons *not* to delegate are few and far between. You might not delegate if you have the greatest expertise and no one else needs to develop that expertise; it's a simple and quick task. One reason leaders often cite for not delegating more is that they don't want to overload their already busy employees. Clearly, there is a fallacy in the manager's assumption here—that adding to the plate will put the individual into overload.

What we have learned about strengths is that adding strength-based accountabilities to an employee's responsibilities will increase engagement, motivation, and energy. So, help your employee by identifying what can come off his plate, what can best be done by someone else. Employees, similar to bosses, can become victims in the delegating game by saying yes to everything so they appear to be "team players" and good employees. If an employee takes this approach, eventually his plate will not overflow with great tasks that make maximum use of his strengths, but stuff he has to get done because, well, it's sitting there on his plate!

Delegate to the employee's strength as much as possible. Be certain to engage him in a dialogue about how this task, responsibility, or accountably fits into his strength—or how it doesn't. Be sure that you aren't in the unenviable position where fewer than 20 percent of your employees have the opportunity to do what they do best every day. Sadly, that data show that we have not yet mastered loading our people with strengths-based work!

If you're operating from a strengths-based approach to management, you will consistently and purposefully delegate to make the greatest use of each staff member's strengths. Makes sense, doesn't it? You've hired an individual for his significant talent (perhaps in an area where you are weak), and he has passion for applying this strength. Why not give him every possible opportunity to develop his strength even further by thoughtfully and appropriately applying it to this situation, at this time? Don't wait until you are certain he can competently handle the task. By then, his growing edge, and perhaps his inspiration, will be gone. Here are some compelling "rules of thumb" about delegation:

1. Delegate *responsibility* by putting others in charge of doing certain activities or tasks.

2. Delegate *authority* by giving others the power to make decisions to carry out tasks or responsibilities.

3. Delegate *accountability* by giving ownership to the appropriate individual for the ultimate outcomes to be achieved.

The "GRASP" Model of Delegating

Not only what you delegate, but how you delegate, influences your employee's success. The GRASP model is an effective structure for discussing any accountability you delegate to your staff.

Goal

Resources

Authority

Standards

Pride

♠ Goal: Communicate the desired end result to create a clear, mutual understanding of what is to be accomplished.

♠ Resources: Corral all resources including time, money, tools, people, and information to support the person in accomplishing the goal.

♠ Authority: Communicate the authority level, as well as any restrictions or constraints that exist, such as the amount of available money or decision-making authority.

♠ Standards: Establish quality guidelines that define how performance and progress will be measured and evaluated. What does excellent performance look like? Employees will become frustrated if these are not defined clearly and communicated well. Also, they will be more empowered and more committed if you decide the standards together.

♠ Pride: Define what will make the employee proud to accomplish the goal. What is the impact of the desired outcome? A compelling answer to this question is highly motivational for the employee.

Where and when will you discover your first opportunity to delegate to your employees' strengths? How will you delegate to build, improve upon, and leverage the strengths of each employee? Don't be bound by job descriptions or the way it's always been done…give yourself and your staff the freedom to expand beyond those shackles and to truly play to each individual's strengths!

100-Percent Responsibility

Despite our best wishes and hopes, life isn't always fair. While none of us can completely control all the circumstances of our lives, we can choose our reaction to those circumstances. We are responsible for our reaction to any situation life throws at us. Choice is at the center of responsibility. We will only be fully accountable and responsible when we recognize that, no matter what happens in our lives, we always have choices.

Gary Gore (no relationship to Vice President Al Gore), president of Team Trek and author of *Navigating Change: A Field Guide to Personal Growth*, built a retreat center in Arkansas where he orchestrates elaborate, powerful simulations for members of corporate groups. Gary's compelling teaching is indisputable. He teaches us that whoever we are or whatever we do, we, and we alone, are 100- percent responsible for our reaction to every situation.[4]

The good news about embracing Gore's teaching is that accepting 100-percent responsibility is extremely powerful. When we accept this as our own truth, accountability happens. Imagine asking yourself, what did I do to create, promote, or allow this situation? during all of the undesirable situations in your work life. This question is action-oriented, and destroys any sense of victim or blame. Perhaps you have a staff member who is not performing as well as you expect. What did *you* do to create, promote, or allow this situation? Our bet is that you will uncover many answers, such as noticing where you have given unclear expectations, seeing the ways in which you let him off the hook and didn't hold him responsible, or remembering the feedback you didn't give him because you didn't want to feel uncomfortable.

One-hundred-percent responsibility is an attitude to help us see we need never fall victim to our circumstances. When we are 100 percent responsible, we are empowered to take charge of this situation and the next. You can decide to outline specific goals and expectations with a staff member who isn't performing well, you can hold him more tightly responsible, and you can choose to give him clearer and more direct feedback.

CREATING AN ENVIRONMENT OF
100-PERCENT RESPONSIBILITY

Do you hear people make excuses or blame others for their failures or delays? Maybe some of these phrases are familiar to you:

- ♠ "I didn't know you needed it right away."
- ♠ "It's not my fault it isn't done."
- ♠ "No one told me to do that."
- ♠ "I didn't get invited to the meeting."
- ♠ "He said he'd get back to me, but he didn't."
- ♠ "I would have had it done, but the people in (insert your favorite target group: accounting, quality, human resources, the Andromeda Galaxy...) didn't get their part done."

These phrases, and similar "reasons," are clues that you have not yet built an environment of personal and team responsibility. And if the team is not 100-percent responsible, it is difficult to sustain team members being accountable to each other. Do you still have team members in the victim mode, not taking full responsibility for their commitments, their performance, or the performance of the team? Can you change this dynamic? You bet you can!

In an environment in which each person is 100-percent responsible and holds him or herself accountable, people can count on each other. The "Responsibility Loop" occurs when we are 100 percent responsible for our actions:

Manager: "The team report is due today. Will I have it on time?"

Bill: "Yes. I realized just yesterday that Carl was on vacation. I needed his data to complete the report, but I worked through that."

Manager: "Oh?"

Bill: "Yes, I knew I was responsible for the report, so I took ownership. I was a little irritated that Carl didn't get me the data before he left, but I realized I was not very clear with him about how important it was. So I let go of the irritation and began to ask around to find out where else the data might be."

Manager: "What did you discover?"

Bill: "I learned that Carl's administrative assistant inputs the data, so she had it! I received it from her last night."

Manager: "Excellent—and what did you learn from your own resourcefulness?"

Bill: "Next time, I will be clearer with others who have inputs for the report, and ask for specific deliverables by a specific date and time."

This is an example of 100-percent responsibility in action. Let's follow the steps in the Responsibility Loop. They are:

1. I have an intention and a commitment to do something for which I am responsible.
2. I recognize there could be glitches.
3. When a glitch happens, I forgive the other person and myself for not having a sound process.
4. I decide what action I can take now—and I take it.
5. I learn from this event for the next time.

It is very intriguing to accept the perspective that I am 100-percent responsible for my response to every circumstance of my life. At first blush, you might think this is a huge burden. You may be overwhelmed thinking, "How can I take all that responsibility onto my shoulders?" The truth is, just the opposite occurs. When I hold myself as 100-percent responsible, I am also 100-percent resourceful. I am empowered to take action and to manage my emotions. I am accountable for my work. I blame no one. I am a victim to no circumstance. How liberating! How powerful!

With 100-percent responsibility as your attitude, "they" are no longer in charge—*you* are! When we accept full responsibility, our work becomes much more interesting. We take pride in our accomplishments because they are truly ours! We learn from our disappointments and mistakes because they are not failures—they are teachers. We can help ourselves and our colleagues move from a life attitude of "victim" to a life attitude of "100 percent responsibility." This shift in life-view and orientation is potent and freeing. To enjoy resurgence in energy, accept 100 percent responsibility as a life attitude. Responsibility begins with each one of us. We cannot, in good faith, hold each other accountable until we hold ourselves responsible. Making this shift in your response and your attitude will alter your organization and your life.

Celebrate...Celebrate...
Dance to the Music!

One of the management processes you'll use more when you lead from a strengths-based approach is the process of recognizing, rewarding, and celebrating the contributions of your staff members. As a matter of fact, when you manage from strengths, the rewards will be much easier to administer—because the reward is inherent in the tasks and accountabilities for which your staff members are responsible. Truly, there will be joy and reward in the work itself!

Nevertheless, reward and recognition are important for a leader who seeks to ante up—to invest in processes to build a stronger foundation of strengths. Rewarding positive action and celebrating accomplishments builds team spirit and self-confidence in your employees. By celebrating the accomplishments of staff members, you foster pride, self-esteem, and further commitment. Not bad for something that's also easy and fun!

To celebrate your employees as they achieve from their strengths, be sure to make the celebrations meaningful. This isn't too hard if your intention is to convey appreciation and value. All you need do is:

1. Actively seek out opportunities for celebration, both large and small.

2. Ensure that the act of celebrating is an active and regular part of your team meetings.

3. Use celebrations and rewards that people value.

Rewards—monetary or not—are best managed when they are given for explicit behaviors or results, and are understood by the recipient. Rewards work best if they are meaningful to the recipient, so managers need to ask employees about their favorite rewards and celebrations. A pizza party may work great for one employee—and a half-day off may be Nirvana to another!

You'll find it's easy to apply rewards, recognition, and celebrations in a strengths-based environment! The focus is not only on the accomplishment itself, but also on acknowledging, articulating, and underscoring the demonstrated strength that led to the results. At B2B Printers, Michael celebrated with Anna when she successfully shepherded her new sales analysis process through the approval path and implemented it in the new quarter. Michael acknowledged Anna's result—implementation of the new process—and he acknowledged her strength in achieving it: her ability to analyze, conceptualize, and design a new and strategic tool.

What's immensely powerful about applying strengths to rewards, recognition, and celebration is that employees are acknowledged for who they *are*—not just what they have *done*. They will take sincere recognition of their strengths to heart—and they will clearly know the competencies they should continue to apply. And the bonus? Those are also the competencies they most *want to* apply—the ones that allow them to say, "Yes, I do what I do best every day!"

Development

The final management process we address in this chapter is developing your employees. By now, you probably have excellent ideas about how to accomplish meaningful development when operating from a strengths-based approach. Development will be fierce, inspired, targeted, and fun when it is strength-based. You'll experience less resistance and more motivation when an employee attends a course to learn a new tool or process in an area of strength, instead of a skill in an area of weakness. For you golfers among our readers, this is like taking a putting class versus a budgeting class. An entirely different level of motivation is at play!

Aligning your training and other development activities to strengths also leverages your development dollars. It's like taking a good brand and expanding it to another line of products. By building on the strengths that exist in your group, you're transforming good employees into outstanding ones, and excellent employees into superb ones. What other actions will leverage your resources so highly?

How do you shift yourself and your staff from a weakness-based to a strengths-based focus? It may not be intuitively obvious. You may recall these questions from Chapter 4♠, when you asked them of yourself:

- ♠ What is your employee's strength that the two of you choose to develop?
- ♠ Who can he talk to, to learn more about this strength?
- ♠ What might she read to expand her competence in this strength?
- ♠ How can he educate himself more in this strength?
- ♠ Who will she partner with to complement her strength?

Let's see if we can be more specific. Anna has the strength of visioning. Visioning is the strength that enables her to sort through the clutter, identify a specific need, find the best route to achieve it, and then look around the next corner for additional paths that are likely to be successful. This is not a skill that can easily be taught. It is a distinct way of thinking, a special perspective on the world. This perspective allows Anna to see patterns where others see only complexity and chaos.

To help Anna become even more grounded in her visioning strength, Michael and Anna set these development objectives:

♠ Partner with Kel, who has a strength of putting ideas into action. Kel's need for action, and Anna's perspective on the best path to take, makes for a powerful partnership. Anna commits to hold a conversation with Kel, by April 30, about possibilities for the two of them to partner.

♠ Read a visionary, forward-looking book, such as *The World is Flat* by Thomas L. Friedman (Picador, 2007), and apply his ideas to our sales process. Document thoughts for making this happen, and share them with Michael by May 31.

♠ Join the Sales Forms Task Force, which has been bogged down in creating a vision of how their process could be better. After understanding their goals, guide them in creating a meaningful vision of the desired state of sales forms. Complete this by the end of Q2.

Michael also took an assignment to assist Anna with her development. He will talk to some of his peers—other sales directors with different accountabilities by geography and industry—to determine if they can use Anna's strength in analysis, because she is eager to do more in this area. Her colleagues in other departments could likely benefit from this strength, because B2B Printers has typically hired for sales experience; that is, before they learned about strengths. Furthermore, this action would give Anna, and ultimately her peers, more visibility into the challenges faced by other sales professionals—and thus a greater knowledge of the entire sales process in B2B.

Do you get a sense of how to make this real for your organization? When we focus on strengths development, we seem to be much less inclined to seek courses and classroom work as development strategies. This is really good news, because on-the-job development activities are more interesting, tangible, and powerful than classes, and the transference back to work is immediate and sustainable.

Implementation Ideas

To realign your management processes at work and make them strengths-based:

HIRE FOR STRENGTHS

To create a strengths-based approach to hiring, look at the work your department accomplishes now and anticipates in the future, from the deeper perspective of strength. Ask yourself (your staff can help) what inherent strengths are imperative for accomplishing our accountabilities both now and in the future? Then post, interview, and hire for those strengths.

MANAGE PERFORMANCE BASED ON STRENGTHS

When onboarding and managing performance throughout an employee's tenure in a role, build on his strengths by asking that all-important question: What does my employee need now to ensure success in applying his strengths? Set SMART goals that engage the employee's strengths and apply them more broadly and deeply to the needs of the organization. Be sure to instill excellent processes to provide frequent feedback on performance goals. Monitor progress and check content frequently to ensure that the goals are still accurate, engaging, and benefiting the employee, the department, and the organization.

DELEGATE TO BUILD STRENGTHS

When you delegate to an employee's strength, use GRASP to be sure that you both know the Goal, Resources, Authority level, Standards of excellence, and Pride inherent in accomplishing the responsibility.

REWARD, RECOGNIZE, AND CELEBRATE

Begin by surveying your group to find out how they prefer to be acknowledged (you may already know this). Does the group enjoy social events? Do most people seem to prefer a sincere, verbal acknowledgement at a staff meeting? Do some light up at a hand-written note or an e-mail. Do others beam when you thank them privately or allow them some flexibility in how they manage their days? Build a recognition plan that will work for your team, and celebrate their strengths consistently.

DEVELOP STRENGTHS

In Chapter 4♠, you learned how to build and develop your strengths. The key questions you explored apply here as well, in working with employees:

- ♠ What is your employee's strength that the two of you choose to develop?
- ♠ Who can he talk to, to learn more about this strength?
- ♠ What might he read to expand his competence in this strength?
- ♠ How can he educate himself more in this strength?
- ♠ Who will she partner with to complement her strength?

CLAIM 100-PERCENT RESPONSIBILITY

For an interesting read on this important attitude, pick up Gary Gore's book *Navigating Change: A Field Guide to Personal Growth* (Team Trek, 2002).

SEEK GREAT DEVELOPMENT IDEAS

Good resources for strengths-based developmental ideals come in many forms, including software tools such as PeopleSoft and Forthill, and books such as *The Successful Manager's Handbook* by Susan H. Gebelein, Lisa A. Stevens, Carol J. Skube, and David G. Lee (Personnel Decisions International, 1992), *The Successful Executive's Handbook* by Susan H. Gebelein, Kristie J. Nelson-Neuhaus, and Elaine B. Sloan (Personnel Decisions International, 1999), and *StrengthsFinder 2.0* by Tom Rath (Gallup Press, 2007). Pursue these and other sound resources for development ideas in the areas of strengths.

READ A BIT FROM *Now, Discover Your Strengths*

Read the section titled "One by One" in Chapter 6♠ of Buckingham and Clifton's book, *Now, Discover Your Strengths* (Free Press, 2001) for more ideas on leading and growing others' strengths.

LAUGH A LITTLE—OR A LOT

On a humorous note, we thought you might enjoy some actual descriptions people wrote on accident forms, which were published by the Arizona Safety Association, and reprinted in *The Oz Principle* (Portfolio, 2004). Talk about un-accountability!

- ♠ "Coming home, I drove into the wrong house and collided with a tree I don't have."
- ♠ "A pedestrian hit me and went under my car."
- ♠ "The guy was all over the road. I had to swerve a number of times before I hit him."
- ♠ "I had been shopping for plants all day and was on my way home. As I reached the intersection, a hedge sprang up, obscuring my vision. I did not see the other car."

♠ "As I approached the intersection, a sign suddenly appeared in a place where no stop sign had ever appeared before."

♠ "An invisible car came out of nowhere, struck my vehicle, and vanished."

♠ "The telephone pole was approaching. I was attempting to swerve out of the way when it struck my front end."

Chapter Six
Ace in the Hole: Uncovering Hidden Strengths

Ace in the Hole: Having an ace as a down card. An advantage or resource kept in reserve until an opportunity presents itself.

In the movie *Hoosiers*, high-school basketball coach Norman Dale (Gene Hackman) decides to rehabilitate Shooter (Dennis Hopper), the father of one of the players. Shooter is an idle, n'er-do-well drunk who frequently embarrasses himself and his son in front of their fellow townsfolk. Dale creates an assistant coach role for Shooter, and then purposefully gets himself thrown out of a game, forcing Shooter into leadership. Shooter steps up to the challenge and guides the team to victory. Ultimately, Coach Dale's belief in his assistant leads Shooter to discover his own strengths and build the confidence he needs to turn his life around.

This is great coaching in action! Dale has faith in Shooter's potential, recognizes Shooter's inherent talents, and creates an opportunity for him to play to his strengths. An "ace in the hole" in poker refers to an ace hidden in your down cards, obviously giving you an advantage. Coaching is how you discover the "aces in the hole" on your team—and begin to use them *fully*, creating an advantage for you, the team, and the organization.

A key role of managers is to help others find their strengths and make the most of them. In business, as in sports, having the right player use the right skills and talents in the right position is a leadership essential. We'll go out on a limb and say that coaching is the *only* tool for unlocking an individual's strengths and applying them at work. You can't delegate the "apply your strengths" assignment and expect people to do anything different from before. Coaching is the bridge from an *intellectual* understanding of strengths to a deep, profound, *emotional* understanding of strengths, which is necessary for their application. Coaching skills, which unlock a person's potential, may appear in mentoring conversations, in discussions with a good friend, or, hopefully, in the developmental conversations you have with your employees. It's empowering to coach your employees into full knowledge of their strengths, so they enthusiastically apply themselves to your organization's challenges. Begin evolving a new view of leadership—one that seeks relentlessly for the strengths in others and inspires the best from them. *You* are the key to unlocking this hidden resource of strengths in your team—your "ace in the hole!"

Success Story: Recognizing Strengths

Several years ago, one of Andrea's staff members was not meeting expected results. Sarah didn't get reports done in a timely manner; she was always late on metrics; she was, for all intents and purposes, an administrative disaster. As manager of a small department, she was struggling mightily.

That is, until they found her strength and played to it. Sarah's work as an organization development consultant was outstanding; she was the best on the team; her ability to support her clients was phenomenal. She offered an appropriate mix of humor, questioning, challenge, and support to her colleagues and clients. Andrea began to look for and reinforce Sarah's strengths and, together, they lifted the veil on Sarah's excellence. Sarah came to understand her strengths with great clarity.

First, Sarah and Andrea designed Sarah's job to play to her strengths, and then they created work-arounds to manage her weaknesses. Sarah also improved her administrative skills to an acceptable, though not outstanding, level. Because she felt respected and valued for what she contributed naturally, she was willing to be creative and enthusiastic about learning new skills. Today, her continued success is based on a clear understanding of her strengths, as well as skill in managing her weaknesses. Through the years, Sarah proved capable of greater responsibility, and is a highly successful vice president today.

What Is Coaching?

In his book *Coaching for Performance: Growing People, Performance and Purpose* (NB Publishing, 2002), John Whitmore defines coaching as "Unlocking a person's potential to maximize their own performance. It is helping them to learn rather than teaching them."[1] We also like coach teacher James Flaherty's definition from his book, *Coaching: Evoking Excellence in Others* (Butterworth-Heinemann, 2005). He says coaching is a mutually satisfying relationship based on "mutual trust, mutual respect, and mutual freedom of expression."

We cannot teach people anything; we can only help them discover it within themselves.
—Galileo Galilei

Building relationships such as those Flaherty recommends requires a significant investment of your time and that of your employees. So, what's in it for you as a manager of people? Why should you coach? What are the benefits of this investment to you and your employees?

Through coaching, an employee can enhance her self-awareness, discover her strengths, and deepen her learning. It is a process that builds accountability for performance, strengthens relationships, and removes barriers to performance. A brief summary of the tangible benefits for the manager and individual follow.

Coaching: Benefits for the Manager	Coaching: Benefits for the Individual
♠ You'll spend less time micro-managing and controlling everything because you will be able to trust your employees to contribute their best. ♠ You'll have more time for strategic responsibilities, running interference, and supporting performance. ♠ You'll pave the way to higher levels of effectiveness because you'll have better relationships, commitment to common goals, and accountability. ♠ You'll create a context for difficult performance feedback—it will be easier to deliver and more likely to be heard.	♠ Employees are empowered to take initiative and act on their own. ♠ Employees have a greater sense of freedom to perform, rather than being controlled, dictated to, or pushed. ♠ Employees are no longer blamed or shamed for mistakes, and don't have to walk on eggs. Growth, development, and learning are key themes. ♠ Employees are motivated and inspired by you because you model respectful behavior, good communication, encouragement, and commitment to growth.

"Being" a Coach

In a few pages, we'll explore how to "do" coaching, but first we begin with the foundation—the mindset of coaching. Coaching requires a delicate balance of challenge and support, focus and flexibility, curiosity and deep listening. It is an attitude you step into—a hat you put on—for engaging in a meaningful developmental conversation. It's powerful and satisfying for both parties and, frankly, it's fun! Your job in "being" a coach is to see your employee in all her greatness, both today and tomorrow.

As a matter of fact, here is the shorthand version, the gem of this chapter. If you remember nothing else, remember this: the coach's client—in this case, your employee—is *creative, resourceful, whole, and wise.*[1] That's it. It's the cornerstone of coaching to perceive your employee as creative, resourceful, whole, and wise. She doesn't need answers; she needs the right questions. She doesn't need advice; she'll discover her own resources. She doesn't need to be fixed; she's not broken. She's whole, healthy, and immensely wise. You'll want to be certain you're in that frame of mind as you enter into a coaching discussion with an employee. If you can't be fully present due to distractions, time pressures, or whatever else is going on in your day, don't coach. Take some time to step into "being" a coach, whether that's a minute, or a day, or a weekend away. Prepare yourself for coaching, and create growth, learning, and insight for both you and your employee!

Coaching is a partnership requiring trust, and you build trust by trusting more. If you have clearly outlined the team's direction, trust your staff members to understand and use their best resources to achieve it. Let go of micromanaging and, instead, be a resource for removing obstacles. Act more like a coach than a manager, seeing the inherent gifts in your employees and creating opportunities for them to engage those gifts.

"Doing" Coaching

Now that you're firmly planted in "being" a coach, what do you *do*? The good coach shows compassion for the employee's struggles, builds understanding of her strengths and motives, and facilitates growth and development. There's no format to follow, though we'll provide you with a road map when we introduce the GROW model. First, let's consider the skills you will use when you begin to coach, and in every coaching interaction thereafter. The essential skills of coaching are:

1. Natural curiosity.
2. Powerful questions.
3. Deep listening.
4. Establishing accountability.
5. Self management.
6. Trusting intuition.

THE FIRST SKILL OF COACHING: NATURAL CURIOSITY

Children learn more in their first few years than during any other time in their lives. This fact does not surprise anyone who has spent time with kids—their curiosity is intense and their questions are incessant! Once we overcome our frustration at not having all the answers, their inquisitiveness fascinates us because it is a trait that we, at one time, shared. Sadly, we somehow lost it along the way.

That insatiable sense of curiosity is a trait shared by many of the great men and women who have made or are making a real difference in our world. They ask evocative questions, look for answers, and seek a better way.

Curiosity is also an essential tool of a great coach, used hand-in-hand with the coach's most powerful tool: questioning. We call this *natural* curiosity because it is a skill few of us have to learn—we simply have to remember it. We all had this skill as children, until it was programmed out of us. Imagine a child without the word *why* in his or her vocabulary!

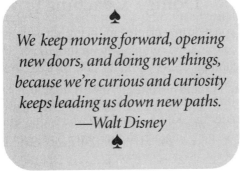

> ♠
>
> *We keep moving forward, opening new doors, and doing new things, because we're curious and curiosity keeps leading us down new paths.*
> —Walt Disney
>
> ♠

While natural curiosity is an important component of high-quality conversations, an interesting tension surrounds it in the business context. We're hired for our knowledge and expertise, not necessarily for our ability to be curious. Too often in business conversations we feel compelled to demonstrate how much we know about an issue, convince others that our point of view is "right," or win the argument. More important, however, is to learn what we don't know, explore our own or others' thinking, and mutually inquire into issues. Our conversations fall on a spectrum based on the degree of curiosity present:

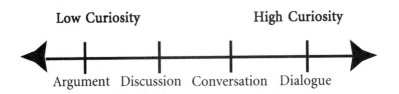

Low Curiosity   **High Curiosity**

Argument   Discussion   Conversation   Dialogue

Arguments are indicative of low curiosity; real dialogue reflects a high level of curiosity. It's that curiosity—and the skill of asking questions—that can truly make our conversations meaningful and rich, leading to better results and greater satisfaction at work. If you have argumentative relationships, try ramping up your natural curiosity; it will have a big affect.

Curiosity is a skill and a mindset. It's a way in which we approach the coaching conversation. Coaching helps the employee uncover and understand her internal motivations, perspectives, and ideas. The curiosity of a great coach is marked by a natural inquisitiveness about the other person's life, wonder about her goals and aspirations, and concern for her level of balance, satisfaction, and fulfillment. To be curious as a coach is a very child-like behavior. It is to marvel at what gems can be mined in the employee's thought processes. When we operate from a place of curiosity, the conversation slows down and goes deep. When an employee says, "I can't do that!" the naturally curious place in us wonders:

- ♠ What led her to that belief?
- ♠ What data is she using?
- ♠ Is she saying that because she doesn't want to do it, or does she feel she can't do it?
- ♠ What barriers does she perceive will thwart her?
- ♠ How does it look different from her perspective than from where I sit?
- ♠ What would be possible if we assumed we could do it, and start from there?
- ♠ What does she feel about it. Is she excited, anxious, worried, intrigued?

This sort of natural curiosity is something we have learned to turn off in a working world driven by extremely fast access to information and nearly as fast requirements to make decisions about it. This kind of curiosity invites the employee into a safe and deep exploration of the issue at hand, an exploration that always reveals additional perspectives and treasures.

When using the skill of curiosity, be curious about what's inside the employee that even *she* hasn't seen yet, because she hasn't had a safe and structured way to explore it. Be curious about her underlying assumptions, beliefs, and values. You'll learn a great deal about your employee, which will help you manage her better in all aspects of her work. Even more important, she'll learn a lot more about herself, which will improve her effectiveness.

Be curious about possibilities, about perspectives, about options, about ideas, about insights, and about barriers. Any time you hear yourself think, "Oh, she probably assumes X," you have a natural avenue for your curiosity to surface! Find out what she really does assume!

Curiosity is not a skill used to drive *your* agenda. It is not curious to wonder things such as, "Why doesn't she see it my way," or, "When is she ever going to get her act together?" Can you see how curiosity from that place is judgmental and will harm your relationship? Your natural curiosity helps your employee to better understand her inner drives and beliefs that support or curtail excellence in her performance. Coaching is curiosity about her, with her, and for her.

To be effective in this naturally curious place, practice detachment— not being committed or attached to any particular solution. When we coach an employee, we may be committed to her gaining as much insight and learning as she can from the conversation, but that's about all we can be attached to. How she does it, how she perceives it, the insights she has—none of these are yours. If you find yourself driving to a particular outcome or solution, *you are no longer coaching.* There are times for you to *manage* people to drive a particular decision, and there are times for you to *coach* others to discover their own wisdom and decisions. This is an important distinction! Coaching is all about the other person and her learning.

THE SECOND SKILL OF COACHING: POWERFUL QUESTIONS

Where natural curiosity is the coach's mindset, powerful questions are her tools for illumination. Questioning is the hallmark of coaching and the most visible behavior of a coach, yet it can be a sham without genuine curiosity.

A powerful question can incite an employee to look deep inside herself, tapping her own wisdom. Through powerful questions, you discover what the employee is thinking, what's behind her thinking, how she arrived at his current stance, and from what assumptions or data she is operating. She uncovers these insights, too!

In the coaching relationship, powerful questions have many uses. Questions can invite a person to engage in the discussion at the outset of a coaching conversation. (What's intriguing you today?) Questions can solicit good information, expand concepts, and clarify different perspectives. (What happened when you tried that new tactic, and how is it different from what you usually do?) Questions can gain agreement and, ultimately, turn an enemy into a friend. (How can we respectfully agree to disagree and move into potential solutions?)

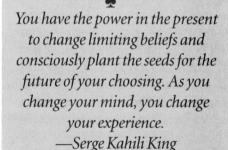

♠

You have the power in the present to change limiting beliefs and consciously plant the seeds for the future of your choosing. As you change your mind, you change your experience.
—Serge Kahili King

♠

Powerful questions are open-ended questions—questions that cannot be answered with a yes or a no. By using open-ended questions, you can draw out the employee's reasoning. This allows you, as a coach, to listen for a new understanding to emerge. The most important benefit of powerful questioning is that it allows us to acquire *more* information, perspective, and data from which to make decisions or plans.

Powerful questions open dialogue, rather than narrowing it to a solution. The results of powerful questions can be high-impact: better discussions, problems solved quickly, and work accomplished with ease. Powerful questions work!

---

12 Always-Great Questions

1. What do you want?
2. How did you create, promote, or allow this situation?
3. If you knew you could not fail, what would you do?
4. Where are your fears?
5. If you knew the answer, what would it be?
6. What is most challenging about this situation?
7. What do you gain from your perspective?
8. What do you notice in your body right now?
9. WHat will you say no to in order to say yes?
10. What do you know to be true?
11. How are you getting in your own way?
12. What else?

People who ask great questions also pause to listen and reflect. Their conversations are more meaningful. They enjoy discussions that enhance their understanding of customers, the marketplace, the environment, and one another. Their dialogues naturally fill with openness and humor; thus, they can diffuse defensiveness by laughing good-naturedly at themselves.

INEFFECTIVE QUESTIONS

Certain types of questions can backfire. These questions do not accomplish our intent, and they can damage your relationship with the other person and hurt their self-esteem or morale. Imagine a boss, reviewing performance on a task with her employee, asking in a belittling tone, "Why did you do it *that* way?" Or, the same boss asking, "Do you *really* think you did a *good* job?" The inherent ridicule in these questions is exacerbated by a cavalier attitude and sarcasm. This approach shuts off valuable input from the employee now and in the future, causing her to retreat, and possibly driving "creative sabotage" later on. This is not coaching.

Another ineffective question is one that is "loaded" from the beginning with the answer already assumed, such as, "Don't you agree that…?" The built-in bias to that question allows virtually no insight from the other person. Other questions that make us wince when we hear them include, "Do you understand what I'm telling you?" and, "Didn't you hear me tell you not to do that?" These are condescending and patronizing, particularly if they are asked with a tone of scolding or an air of importance or authority. These types of questions tend to make us feel small, disrespected, and demoralized.

Open-ended questions are not the easiest to ask. Many of us have not developed powerful skills in drawing people out. It's not surprising, because our indoctrination to close-ended questions began in the American school system when our teachers fired questions in the classroom, one after the other, expecting a quick, short, and correct answer. Closed-ended questions are effective for determining if others have the "right" answers—and for speeding up the lesson plan—but not for engaging them in dialogue! Closed-questions are effective only when you really do need a yes or no answer, a commitment, or a specific piece of information.

To summarize, the purpose of powerful questions is always to increase the learning of the person you are coaching. Powerful questions:

♠ incite introspection and reflection.

♠ increase perspectives and options for the employee.

♠ deepen learning.

♠ lead to deeper and more creative thinking.

♠ help to surface assumptions and beliefs.

♠ expand self-awareness.

♠ forward action.

♠ evoke clarity, discovery, insight, and commitment.

The Implementation Ideas section at the end of this chapter contains additional resources and more examples of powerful questions for your coaching.

THE THIRD SKILL OF COACHING: DEEP LISTENING

Listening is such a simple task, and yet it truly is a complex skill! We want to share a perspective that will make it easier for you to listen more effectively, a skill that is especially important as a leader. Not all listening requires the same intensity and focus, as you know from family gatherings when Uncle Herman bends your ear. While we learn in management courses how to paraphrase and restate.

Listening is a magnetic and strange thing, a creative force. The friends who listen to us are the ones we move toward. When we are listened to, it creates us, makes us unfold and expand.
—Karl Menninger

What we don't learn is that there are different perspectives we can hold about listening—and that each is appropriate in specific circumstances. We call these perspectives "territories" to clarify the different places from which you can listen. You can decide what territory to listen from...it's *your* choice!

Listening From the "Me" Territory

In the Me territory, listening is all about *you*. You are listening to understand the impact of the speaker's comments on you. This is absolutely appropriate in specific situations. For example, when the waiter is telling you tonight's specials—you are best served if you listen from the Me territory. What do I want to eat? What sounds intriguing and interesting? How well will that dish fill my personal commitments to diet? How satisfying does that sound? Unfortunately, for some of us, this is the *only* territory we inhabit.

Listening From the "Thee" Territory

The Thee territory is all about the *other* person. In this place, you listen intently. You are completely engaged with the other person. You aren't writing e-mails or formulating your response, or even thinking about what impact the other person is having on you. You are over there with her, in the moment, 100 percent. You are listening for what she says—and what she doesn't say. You are listening for values, passion, strengths, motivation, beliefs, fears, and emotions. You are listening to the words, and you want to hear the words very clearly (this is where paraphrasing can be useful). Plus you are listening to *more* than the words. You are listening to the feeling, the emotions, the beliefs, and the thought process behind the words.

The Thee territory is an excellent perspective for coaching. In the Thee territory, you help the other person acknowledge her strengths and weaknesses, to look inside for her own answers, and to find new ideas and options. The Thee territory is often just what an employee (or a family member) needs.

Listening From the "We" Territory

In the We territory, you interact with the other person and notice, at a concentrated or heightened level, the affect you are having on her. The We territory is all about the relationship. In the We territory, when you say, "I know you are competent to do this!" you notice how it lands with the other person, that is, if she truly hears it. If you ask, "What actions are you going to take next?" you notice if you have inspired—or scared—her. The We territory calls for extreme honesty and clarity of communication. The We territory is a very powerful place from which you can create authentic and meaningful dialogue. In the We territory, you take full responsibility for both sides of the communication.

All three territories are absolutely appropriate in different circumstances; you choose which one fits the situation. You wouldn't interact with your dry cleaner, most likely, from the Thee or the We territories. However, you might find yourself in the We territory with a teenager who is gaining some maturity about how she interacts with you.

The Territorial Barriers

What gets in the way of listening from each territory? There are simple, common barriers to listening in each of the three territories:

1. Preparing what I want to say (instead of listening).
2. Predicting what the person is going to say (instead of listening).
3. Allowing myself to be bored with the other person (yes, instead of really listening!).

Overcoming these barriers to listening is also simple. First, notice from which territory you are listening. Many of us default to the Me territory, which is often quite inappropriate for work interactions. Consciously choose to go to the Thee territory, and perhaps to the We territory, to deepen the conversation.

Give yourself a moment to prepare your response. Listen fully, and then take a 10-second pause. Take as long as you need to think through what you want to say. This silence is impressive. You may even want to ask for permission to take a moment. The other person will appreciate this action, because it means you are listening fully.

Practice all three territories. Sit and have a conversation with a friend or family member, and consciously choose to listen from the Me, Thee, and We territories. Observe what you notice. How is the dialogue different? What do you hear when you are in each territory? What is the impact on you and the other person when you listen from each territory? (If you don't want to appear schizophrenic, you might want to tell the other person what you're up to!)

If your partner in conversation begins to digress or go into extraneous detail, gently jump in with a question that bridges back to the topic at hand, such as, "What was the impact of the bold move you made?" When we truly stay focused on the other person with ears, eyes, and attention, it's hard to get bored.

You can choose the level you listen from—it is not only your right, but also your responsibility. Making a conscious choice about how you listen lets *you* decide the most effective use of your time and energy, because *you* control the listening territory. You also know your natural default territory. Recognize it and ask yourself, "Which territory will serve me best for this interaction? Which territory do I choose for this interaction?"

THE FOURTH SKILL OF COACHING: ESTABLISHING ACCOUNTABILITY

Establishing individual accountability is perhaps the skill you know best, because you already are an effective leader. The twist in the coaching scenario is this: *You* don't establish the accountability; rather, the employee you're coaching does! She sets it and you support it. You may want to challenge her to set an accountability that is bigger or smaller, or sooner or later. But you want her to set an individual accountability that she will accomplish and feel good about. You want her to have success! You then build on those successes and give her a clear opportunity to see the strengths that contributed to them.

If she slips at her own self-set accountability, she'll learn a great deal, too! And, because it was her accountability, there will be no latitude for blaming you. In the coaching session that would naturally follow a missed accountability, you could explore meaningful questions such as:

♠ What got in your way?

♠ If you could redo it, what would you do differently?

♠ How were you applying your strengths?

♠ What have you learned?

♠ What will you do different next time?

♠

A good leader inspires others with confidence in him or her; a great leader inspires them with confidence in themselves.
—Unknown

♠

Establishing individual accountability creates an external structure that supports and empowers the employee to achieve her goals. The employee holds herself accountable—you are simply the recipient when she reports back. Establishing accountability is simple. The formula lies in the answer to a three-part question:

1. What are you going to do?
2. By when will you do it?
3. How will I know?

There go the people.
I must follow them,
for I am their leader.
—Mahatma Gandhi

As you can see, this formula puts all the responsibility and accountability squarely on the shoulders of the right person—the coachee who is creating it. You might challenge the employee, or perhaps offer additional accountabilities, but it isn't your prerogative to set the accountability. This is not about delegating; rather, it's about assisting the employee to grow and develop.

THE FIFTH SKILL OF COACHING: SELF-MANAGEMENT

The skill of self-management provides you with some great clues about how to manage your own natural tendencies (and perhaps even your natural strengths) in service to the individual you are coaching. Because the agenda for coaching belongs to the employee, it's your job to monitor your own opinions, beliefs, feelings, and judgments. Coaching is not about you, the coach.

The coaching conversation is completely in support of the growth and development of the employee you're coaching. These recommendations can help:

♠ **Manage your ego.** While we want to appear knowledgeable and credible in conversations, *this* conversation has *nothing* to do with how much you know, how clever you are, or how good you look. There's no need to parade your skills and expertise; they are irrelevant here. In fact, they will inhibit learning for the employee if you let them interfere with your natural curiosity, powerful questioning, and deep listening. Coaching is seldom the place in which you teach or demonstrate. Your experience and knowledge offer value to this coaching conversation by leading you to ask more insightful and powerful questions.

♠ **Manage your impatience.** Coaching is not for quick learning. Rather, it is for deep, unequivocal, "in the bones" learning. Allowing the employee to "sit in the question" is often the most powerful thing you can do. For example, Carol gave Tony a weekend assignment to consider how he was contributing to the ongoing problem with his colleague, Perry. She requested that he get back to her on Monday. Carol could just as easily have said, "Tony, you are impatient with Perry and it shows in how you speak to him." However, that statement would have been all about Carol and her own judgments of Tony. When she asked Tony to look for his own answer—and was patient enough to give him time to really consider the question—the learning on Tony's part was huge! He saw ways in which he was contributing to the problem that he had never sensed before, and—here's the gem—that Carol hadn't seen either! The wisdom—and the answer—truly *was* inside Tony. Carol's job was simply to hold him as creative, resourceful, whole, and wise. During a coaching conversation, manage your impatience and create lots of time and space for your employee to reflect upon your powerful question.

♠ **Manage your need to have it be right.** This one is challenging—especially when you are coaching an employee—because if the employee makes a mistake, it can reflect badly on her, the team, you, and the entire department. If we coach to deepen learning, always doing it "right" is highly ineffective. While you may want to reign things in if the action is heading in an illegal direction or safety is a factor, these are literally the *only* times to do so. You don't want to "protect" your employee from making mistakes; mistakes are powerful learning tools. You'll have a great opportunity for further coaching if the employee does—or does not—make a mistake! Either way, there's lots of fodder for deep, unequivocal learning. Typically, it is coaches who are fearful of the employees making mistakes. Let it go. You and the employee don't need to do it perfectly; you need to create learning.

♠ **Manage your agenda.** We mentioned earlier that, if you find yourself driving your own solution, your own way of addressing the problem, or your own great idea, you are no longer coaching. The staff member's agenda drives the coaching. What does she want and need next? What will create greater learning and effectiveness? There are times and places for you to manage the agenda, whether you are training people in a particular skill, or educating them about the actions that came from last week's executive meeting. But, not during coaching. This can be challenging because, as a manager, you *do* have an agenda for your employee. You need her to perform at her best. Without that agenda, you wouldn't be investing the time to coach. However, your agenda is a *big* agenda. If your employees agree to your agenda of excellence in performance and engagement, *how* excellence specifically shows up in their work is *their* decision, in alignment with the overall vision and goals.

♠ **Manage your growth.** You cannot effectively coach if you are not growing. No kidding! Not only is it important for you to model growth and development, it's also important to enhance your empathy for the learner you are coaching. Most important of all, coaching presents you with challenging and unique situations. You'll always be learning during coaching and between sessions. You'll be thinking, "how might I have made that question more powerful?" or," I stopped listening there for a while—what took me away from this conversation?" If there are other leaders around you who are also learning to coach, you might find it helpful to swap insights.

Which of these self-management skills do you anticipate will pose the greatest challenge for you? These skills can be tough to control because some of them have already proven effective for you and have contributed to your success. In the context of coaching, though, they can trip you up! Learn to manage yourself to be the best coach you can be!

THE SIXTH SKILL OF COACHING: TRUSTING INTUITION

We include intuition as one of the six essentials skills of coaching because there isn't a precise plan to follow when coaching. Unlike a structured training event or a detailed process flow, intuition guides you in asking powerful questions and engaging in deep listening. Intuition is an inner knowing, an inner seeing, and an inner sensing. It is often referred to as our sixth sense. Some perceive intuition as illogical or irrational. Recent studies suggest that intuition may be the skill of very quickly organizing all the available data into a pattern.[2] Merriam-Webster Online Dictionary defines intuition as "the power or faculty of attaining to direct knowledge or cognition without evident rational thought and inference."

Coaches are more effective when they can access their intuition. How do you experience your intuition? Many people experience it physically. You may feel a knot in your stomach, sense heat in your chest or shoulders, or find your foot moving. Some people hear their intuition through words. Some people see their intuition as a picture or an image. It might be a metaphor, such as seeing their coachee pushing a big box up a hill. Or it might be a clear picture of what is next, such as seeing the individual in a meeting with the new client.

Similar to any new skill, recognizing intuition is a muscle that can be developed with practice and flexing. Accessing your intuition is a skill you can hone. Your natural curiosity may also give you potent clues to your intuition. If you find yourself suddenly thinking, "I wonder if she's feeling unsupported," that might be your intuition talking to you!

It is simple to express your intuition. Try the words, "I have a hunch that..." or, "I wonder if..." Imagine you have seen, in your mind's eye, the picture of your employee pushing and straining against a big box. You might express your intuition in this way: "I have a hunch that you see this as a challenging task. How do you see it?" or, "I wonder if this is going to require a lot of pushing on your part. What's your sense?" or even, "In my mind, I see you pushing against a big box. Does that have any meaning for you? What?"

One final point: Intuition is never wrong. You may say something that doesn't land right; the action you take may not have the effect you expect. But the fact that you experience the inner wisdom is never wrong. Just saying it aloud allows the coachee the freedom to go where she needs to go. On a personal note, in training to be a coach, Andrea discovered that her intuition often came out in her humor. She'd be working with a coachee and say something she thought was a bit off the wall, indicative of her dry humor. In all cases, her humor suggested an appropriate powerful question or action. After years of paying closer attention to her intuition, in the split second between when she first hears the words of a funny little quip and when she says it aloud, Andrea has learned to trust that this may be her intuition giving her some useful information or insight. She then chooses her words based upon the effect she wants to have on the person she is coaching.

Speaking your intuition sets the stage for open, candid dialogue and potentially rich introspection for the coachee. It is a powerful tool for exploring the employee's agenda in the coaching conversation. And, believe it or not, it's fun!

A Road Map: Coaching Using the GROW Model

Many leaders, when coaching, find that John Whitmore's GROW model is useful as a road map.[3] The GROW model's four steps provide direction and structure for your powerful questions and listening:

Goals

Reality

Options

Way forward

1. GOALS

Open the coaching session with questions about the employee's goals for the topic at hand. You may spend a significant amount of time here, if your employee is not clear about her goals. So go ahead—

171

linger! This time will help her gain clarity, providing greater direction and inspiration to move forward. Some powerful questions to help you coach for clear goals are:

- ♠ What is your goal?
- ♠ What do you want to accomplish?
- ♠ What is your desired outcome?
- ♠ How will you know when you've achieved this outcome?
- ♠ Which goals are compelling?
- ♠ What would make you feel this time was well spent?
- ♠ What would you like to leave here with?

2. REALITY

Your next step on the coaching road map is current reality. The purpose here is to clarify reality and discover, for the coachee, the "truth" about her situation. What's true and what's not? How different might the reality of this situation look from someone else's point of view?

Try these reality coaching questions to help the coachee understand what is occurring now:

- ♠ What's working well? What's not working well?
- ♠ What are your assumptions? Which assumptions are false?
- ♠ What are your expectations?
- ♠ What have you tried so far? With what success?
- ♠ What's missing that could make a difference?
- ♠ What other information might be useful?
- ♠ What is confusing you?
- ♠ In what area are you stuck in an old pattern?
- ♠ What concerns you most?
- ♠ What unintended results are you getting? How are you contributing to them?

172

♠ When/how often does this happen?

♠ What are the obstacles as you see them?

♠ What are your beliefs about this situation?

♠ What are the implications of this situation? The impact? The ramifications?

♠ What else is important?

3. OPTIONS

This step of the coaching process can be quite fun, as you build and expand the possibilities. With your staff member, generate options, perspectives, and ideas; for example, when coaching an executive, Jeffrey, on work/life balance, Carol spent a lot of time in options. Together, they explored the current perspective he had on balance in the current reality: "It's hard to do, with all the pressures from work and home." Once Carol and Jeffrey clearly saw the perspective that he was dearly holding on to, she invited him to "try on" some *different* perspectives that he might have about balance, including: "This is going to be fun, and I've needed more fun lately!" "Balance is easy!" "Balance is vital." They explored the perspective of "Balance is bad. I should put all the time I possibly can into my work and abandon balance," but he quickly forgot about that thought! He realized that balance is "what I really, really want."

You get the idea! Eventually, Jeffrey chose to shift his perspective on balance from "It is hard to do" to, "I get to feel better about myself and have fun doing it!" From here, they generated a virtual panoply of options about how he could create balance:

♠ Leave work early.

♠ Don't work on Fridays.

♠ Take the entire summer off.

♠ Say no to any meetings after 5 p.m.

♠ Work late on Monday nights and be home by 6 p.m. the rest of the week.

173

- ♠ Take only novels on the airplane.
- ♠ Exercise in the morning/exercise in the evening.
- ♠ Exercise with my daughter on Thursdays and Saturdays.
- ♠ Take my wife away for a weekend without the kids once each quarter.
- ♠ Keep my Blackberry on all weekend/keep it off all weekend.

As you can imagine, coaching from the place of options is exhilarating. You are diverging before you converge. You're creating a vast array of topics but, more importantly, you're opening up your coachee to many more possibilities in how she perceives and thinks about situations. To generate more options, ideas, and possibilities, try some of these questions:

- ♠ What are the possibilities?
- ♠ If you had free choice in the matter, what would you do?
- ♠ What might you do next time?
- ♠ If you do this, what affect will it have?
- ♠ What other ideas do you have?
- ♠ What are some crazy ideas?
- ♠ What perspective are you coming from?
- ♠ What's another perspective you could try? And another?
- ♠ How can you use your strengths more?
- ♠ How else could someone handle this?
- ♠ What's another idea? And another?
- ♠ What would be helpful to brainstorm?
- ♠ What other angles can you think of?
- ♠ Who could you ask to gather a new perspective on possibilities?

♠ What other possibilities might there be?

♠ If you had a magic wand, what would you do?

♠ What else might you do?

♠ What are other ways you might get what you want/ need?

♠ What are you overlooking?

♠ How does the goal have to change for success?

4. THE WAY FORWARD

In the final step, The Way Forward, ask the employee what specific action she will take, by when, and how you will know it has been accomplished, thereby establishing accountability. To gain this commitment, try these questions:

♠ Which of these options is most interesting/ compelling/juicy to you?

♠ Which are you willing to do?

♠ Which one do you choose to act on first?

♠ If you do this, will you have met your goals?

♠ What is the first step you will take? What's the next?

♠ What are you going to do? When are you going to do it?

♠ How will this commitment help you obtain your goal?

♠ What might stop you from acting on this commitment?

♠ How could you minimize the obstacles?

♠ What support might you need?

♠ On a scale of one to 10, what degree of certainty do you have that you will follow through on your commitment (one being low and 10 being high)?

♠ What would you need to change in order to increase your rating to a 10?

♠ Who else needs to be involved?

♠ Who else would like to be involved?

♠ What other resources are available to you?

♠ How will you know, along the way, what is being accomplished?

♠ What is your action plan?

♠ What is your back-up plan?

♠ What resources do you need?

♠ What support can I provide?

While GROW is a road map, the distance between the four steps may not be even. In one conversation, you may spend a lot of time on Goals or Reality, while in another coaching interaction you'll focus on the Options phase or the Way Forward. You may also cycle through the road map a few times in one conversation. Sometimes you'll do the steps out of order. Most of the time, however, the GROW model is an excellent guide for forwarding the coaching conversation while creating accountability for action.

Coaching, Ever Expanding

As you become more confident in your coaching skills, you'll find situations in which you want to coach more. Great! You can expand the depth of the coaching relationships that you've already established by broadening the topics to include career, authenticity, leadership, balance, health, meaning, and purpose. If you want to enter more coaching relationships with team members, be sure to explain what coaching is, and don't forget to ask permission to coach. Use GROW to help guide you through the actual conversations. Practice your coaching skills in all conversations, and you'll discover that you are building trust and respect across the organization.

Back to That Hammer-and-Nail Conversation...

Coaching is a great tool for managers who want to build strong relationships; however, coaching is not always the perfect tool! You wouldn't use a hammer to open a wine bottle (well, maybe if you were desperate!). There's a time and a use for every tool. When should you use your coaching skills—and when are the tried and true management skills of setting goals, delegating, informing, deciding, and training the right tools to use? One of the mistakes we see leaders make, once they have acquired a basic coaching skill set, is to use coaching in *all* situations. Certain criteria need to be met for successful coaching to occur:

♠ Have you negotiated for coaching? Is the employee ready to engage in the dialogue inherent in a coaching interaction? Does she know her responsibility in the coaching relationship?

♠ The staff member must have sufficient knowledge and understanding about the topic at hand to have a meaningful dialogue with you. There is nothing quite as frustrating as being asked for your opinion when you have little knowledge upon which to base it. Very early in learning a task the employee needs training, not coaching.

♠ The employee must be in a place where learning is a high priority. She must be open and willing to explore a topic from multiple perspectives. If she is anxious and not ready to explore options, you must get her there before you can coach her.

♠ There must be enough time to coach. In two minutes, your staff member will make a presentation to the senior management team. When she asks, "How is Steve going to attempt to sabotage my proposal?" you do not have enough time to coach her in how to read body language; simply answer her question. If you are in a hurry or there is an emergency, it's *not* the right time to coach.

♠ Are you willing to let go of control, to *not* have the answer, and to accept the decision of your employee—because learning is the highest priority right now?

♠ Are you unequivocally holding the employee as creative, resourceful, whole, and wise, right now, in this minute? Coaching is the time to see the employee's strengths and assist her in accessing her inner wisdom. You can do this only if you can see that strength and creativity within her. If you are angry or irritated with her, it may not be a good time to coach.

♠ Coach when the employee's development is your highest priority. There are times when delegation, information dissemination, or training is more appropriate.

We are encouraged that so many organizations see the value of coaching as a leadership tool. It is affirming (for both parties) to coach someone—at the right time. We encourage you to continue learning all you can about how to coach your employees, and then go for it! Use that hammer when a nail presents itself!

Ace in the Hole

Leaders guide others in discovering and applying their strengths at work. This inspires employees to utilize their best talents, catalyzing purposeful action and superlative contributions at the workplace. So, when will you coach your employees to discover their "aces in the hole"? Coaching is something you can begin now, today. You have enough skill. You don't have to go to a class. Nothing in the organization has to change for you to be able to coach your people. We've taken you through the "being" and "doing" of coaching, so you are well-equipped to coach your employees into their strengths. Not only will you unlock your employees' strengths and potential, but as a coach and leader, you will achieve personal reward and renewal while creating greater success for others and for your organization.

Implementation Ideas

To coach your employees to discover and apply their strengths, follow the same steps Michael, of B2B Printers, completed. We've summarized them here, or you can refer back to the Implementation Ideas at the end of Chapters 2♠, 3♠, and 4♠.

Begin by telling your staff about the work you've been doing to discover and apply your own strengths. Ask them to read *Play to Your Strengths,* and talk about how you would like them to be able to use their strengths every day, for their own satisfaction and for the good of the organization!

Employees Discover Their Strengths

INVITE EMPLOYEES TO LIST THEIR STRENGTHS

Invite your employees to list all possible strengths, skills, and passions. The following "Your Core Strengths" diagram can help.

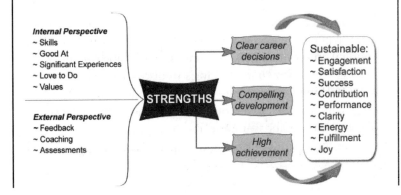

Some useful questions include:

- ♠ What do I excel at?
- ♠ What is easy for me?
- ♠ What do I enjoy?
- ♠ What am I passionate about?
- ♠ What have I done well in the past, but no longer have the opportunity to do?
- ♠ What do I believe I might do well, but have never had the chance to try?

COMPLETE TWO HELPFUL TOOLS

Have them complete the Clifton StrengthsFinder and the VIA Signature Strengths Questionnaire to help them name their strengths. Encourage them to ask others to add to their list of strengths.

"BUCKET" STRENGTHS

Have them group their strengths into "buckets" or categories that represent their deepest and most powerful strengths, and assign a name to each strength, making it more tangible and real. Remind them to create no more than five named strengths.

NOTICE STRENGTHS

Throughout a two-week period, invite them to simply notice when they become engaged, enthused, excited, inspired, intrigued, or passionate! These emotional reactions offer important clues to our deepest strengths.

COACH THEM TO STRENGTHS

Coach them individually about what they are learning about their strengths. Some helpful questions:

- ♠ What are you learning about your strengths?
- ♠ What is intriguing and interesting about discovering your strengths?
- ♠ What situations call for you to use your strengths?

Employees Apply Their Strengths

ALIGN ROLES WITH STRENGTHS

In a coaching session, explore how well the employee's role aligns with her strengths. Some valuable questions:

- ♠ How well does your current role align with your strengths?
- ♠ How might you create more opportunity to use your strengths in your current role?
- ♠ Is your current role the best it can be for playing to your strengths, or does it need to shift in some way?
- ♠ How might you change your current role, adding or eliminating responsibilities so that you can apply your strengths more completely every day?
- ♠ How can you build and enhance your strength so that you're even better at it?
- ♠ How can I help you as your manager?

SUPPLEMENT WITH STRENGTHSFINDER 2.0

If your employees have used the Clifton StrengthsFinder, you may want to purchase a copy of *StrengthsFinder 2.0:* from Gallup's *Now, Discover Your Strengths* by Tom Rath (Gallup Press, 2007)—a handy reference book for contributing great ideas about how to build on strengths.

Employees Discover Their Weaknesses

TALK ABOUT WEAKNESSES

Introduce the concept of weakness, if it hasn't already come up in conversation. Create a safe space for doing this—it can be challenging for employees to claim their weaknesses to their boss! If you are uncertain that there is enough safety for the employee to do this with you, you might ask her to do the exercise on her own. Here's a way to position weaknesses:

Since developing our strengths is based in part on acknowledging and accepting our weaknesses, it's helpful to take a frank look at weaknesses. Once we acknowledge and accept our weaknesses, we can move on to the exciting challenge of working fully from our strengths. To be sure, many of us know the things we put off and the things we do not enjoy. Only rarely, though, do we admit that those are actually weaknesses! I encourage you to identify your weaknesses so we can put a plan in place to manage them and, if possible, make them unnecessary to your job!

ASK YOUR STAFF MEMBER TO
IDENTIFY HER WEAKNESSES

These clues can help identify weaknesses:

- ♠ You learn it slowly.
- ♠ You are defensive about it.
- ♠ It lowers your confidence.
- ♠ You have no exciting and compelling future vision for that weakness.
- ♠ You procrastinate doing it.
- ♠ You shy away from it.
- ♠ You agonize over it.
- ♠ It isn't fun.

- ♠ You want to ask for help, or give it to someone else to do.
- ♠ Your inner critic is very vocal.
- ♠ Your neck gets sore, your stomach turns over, your eyes twitch, or your head aches when you think about it or have to do it.

ACKNOWLEDGE AND ACCEPT

Teach them to acknowledge and accept their weaknesses, and introduce them to the weakness management strategies you learned in Chapter 3♠. What weakness can they delegate, purchase, or ignore?

ADDRESS CAREER-LIMITING WEAKNESSES

If there is a career-limiting weakness the employee needs to address and improve to reach an acceptable level of performance, create a development plan together.

FOR YOUR VIEWING PLEASURE

To watch coaching in action, check out these movies: Hoosiers, Sister Act, Dead Poet's Society, Rudy, Dances with Wolves, and Apollo 13.

FOR YOUR READING PLEASURE

We provide some articles about coaching on our Website *(www.play2yourstrengths.com)*. Our favorite books on coaching include:

Co-active Coaching: Coaching People Toward Success in Work and Life by Laura Whitworth, Karen Kimsey-House, Henry Kimsey-House, and Phil Sandahl (Davies-Black, 2nd edition, 2007).

Coaching for Performance: Growing People, Performance and Purpose by John Whitmore (Nicholas Brealey, 3rd edition, 2002)

Coaching: Evoking Excellence in Others by James Flaherty (Butterworth-Heinemann, 1999)

Also, on the topic of intuition, you may enjoy checking out Malcolm Gladwell's book, *Blink* (Little, Brown and Company, 2005).

TRY OUT SOME ADDITIONAL EFFECTIVE, OPEN-ENDED COACHING QUESTIONS

- ♠ What is your most powerful next step?
- ♠ How can you use your strengths to add value today?
- ♠ Which is the greater risk to the success of this situation—doing something or doing nothing?
- ♠ What was behind setting these goals in the first place? What will they gain you?
- ♠ What assumptions do you need to test?
- ♠ How can you see the situation from a different perspective? What does ownership mean?
- ♠ What does it mean to influence?
- ♠ Where do you get in your own way?
- ♠ What does it mean to be creative?
- ♠ Where are you giving your power away? To whom?

Chapter Seven

Dolly Parton:

Completing the

9-to-5 Straight

Dolly Parton: In poker, a straight that includes the five through nine cards ("nine to five").

—*From the 1980 movie* Nine to Five

Less than 24 hours into his parole from a New Jersey penitentiary, charismatic thief Danny Ocean (George Clooney) is already rolling out his next plan. In one night, Danny's handpicked crew of specialists will attempt to steal more than $150 million from three Las Vegas casinos. If you've seen *Oceans Eleven* (the 2001 remake of a 1960 movie of the same name starring Frank Sinatra as Danny Ocean), you know that Danny purposefully picks his crew for their strengths. And his picks are the strongest and best in their respective, and nefarious, fields of expertise. He knows their coordination and ability to work together as a team is paramount to success. As team leader, Danny must orchestrate their work so that each team member—and the team itself—plays to his strengths. There truly is no other way to succeed, whether you're robbing three casinos, or leading a team at work!

This fun, exciting, and, to some, inspiring film shows what you can do when you assemble the right cards. Ocean deals all the cards, with all the right strengths, in just the right order. There cannot be a card missing. He can't leave any gaps. He has to study his cards carefully so he doesn't create a hole in his highly interdependent team. He has to deal a perfect straight.

In poker, a straight is any five consecutive cards. It's a fine metaphor for a team—five cards, aligned, one falling in line with the next, to create a winning hand. As you begin to apply the lens of strengths to your team at work, keep in mind that the strength of the team is not merely the sum of the individuals' strengths. There's one more lens through which to look—the strengths of the team itself. The powerful hand you're holding—all your cards working together, to the team's advantage—represents the team strengths. You hold "A Dolly Parton"—a straight from 9 to 5. Strong teams know the strengths of the individuals and those of the team, and rigorously cultivate and apply them to achieve the team's goals. And, yes, the poker term refers to the hilarious movie *Nine to Five,* starring Jane Fonda, Dolly Parton, and Lily Tomlin as three office workers who scheme to get even with their appallingly chauvinistic boss.

Strong Team Foundation

To build a strong and excellent team, you need a strong foundation comprised of the structures and processes that help to maximize individual team member contributions. Without this foundation, teams falter and never gel. By understanding team development, building trust, setting clear and measured goals and accountabilities, and directly applying team and individual strengths, your team will achieve spectacular results. A strong team accomplishes the work of maturing itself, so it can effectively achieve its goals and vision. A team has at its disposal diversity of thought, a panoply of strengths, and a possibility for synergy that can rise above any loosely formed group of individuals. Impressive power.

It is the work itself that determines whether a *team* is called for— or whether a *group* will do. A group, "a set of interacting individuals who mutually influence each other,"[1] makes perfect sense when the work does not call for high interdependency to achieve goals. For example, accountants supporting different divisions of a business may come together to share ideas and processes, improving overall effectiveness. If their goals are not interdependent—if they do not need to work together to accomplish their performance objectives—a simple group will accomplish the purpose.

When interdependency exists, however, forming a team is ideal for achieving results. A team is "a small group of people with complementary skills committed to a common purpose, a set of specific performance goals, and an approach for which they hold themselves mutually accountable."[2] A team implies significant alignment, commitment, and interdependency among its members. Whether it's a project team, virtual or co-located, ad hoc, or an intact staff, the decision to create and sustain a team is one we make in light of the requirements of the work itself. Creating and sustaining a team is hard work. Don't bother to put forth the effort to create a team when a group is sufficient. However, a team often *is* necessary to meet the complex and sophisticated requirements of internal and external customers in today's world.

Gumby Team Leaders

Remember Gumby, the green character made of pliable rubber wrapped around a wire frame? You can bend and flex Gumby into a wide variety of positions—some strong, some funny, and some, well, downright ridiculous! Gumby maintains his solid and original shape—even when you bend and flex him into strange positions.

As a leader of a team, you are Gumby—bendable, flexible, and resilient. Leadership is changing, because every organization must accomplish more with fewer resources. The demand for flexible leadership is increasing as technology drives rapid change and customers demand instant, customized solutions. As a result, leadership today is much more about influence than authority. Realizing that teams develop through time and don't begin as high-performing entities reinforces the importance of leadership flexibility.

Leaders must develop the ability in themselves and their staff to discern customer needs and to be innovative, responsive, flexible, and comfortable with ambiguity and change.
—Robert J. Lee and Sara N. King

The Team Development Clock

A classic error made by team members and leaders is to assume that high-performing teams happen with the flip of a switch. We bring people together, call them a "team," and immediately expect superior performance. Unrealistic! Only with intention and attention do we build the relationships and the strengths required to create a highly effective team.

It's not in our nature to form immediately into an intimate, open, strong, and high-achieving team. If human nature didn't make it challenging enough, organizational dynamics can also create resistance to "teaming." Reward systems and performance management processes tend to support individual accomplishment over team accomplishment. Typically, individual accomplishment and strength create career success. When we attempt to form strong teams, individuals may mourn the loss of independence, autonomy, and the simple ease they enjoyed working on their own.

Creating a strong team is an investment, a "letting go" of individual autonomy, a new paradigm.

It is amazing what can be accomplished when nobody cares about who gets the credit.
—Robert Yates

Understanding how teams develop and knowing time-honored ways to facilitate their development creates reasonable expectations and helps the team focus its efforts. It's like raising a child; you can't expect him to form full sentences, read and write his name, hold a job, and get a master's degree before his first birthday!

The *Forming-Storming-Norming-Performing* model of team development (page 190) is a widely used representation of team growth and change in the business world today. Bruce Tuckman, who published this theory in 1965, maintained that all four stages are necessary and inevitable for the team to grow, to face up to challenges, to tackle problems, to find solutions, to plan work, and to deliver results. Essentially, this body of work depicts the path teams follow to discover, utilize, and further leverage their strengths.

Historically, there have been four stages in the Tuckman model, though more recently he added a fifth, *Adjourning*. We created a model, the Team Development Clock, to depict Tuckman's first four stages. An apt metaphor, the clock reminds us that it takes time to evolve through the stages and "settle" into our collective strengths. We may find our team circling back to the earlier stages, especially when new members join. In *Oceans Eleven*, you can actually watch Danny's team evolve through these stages.

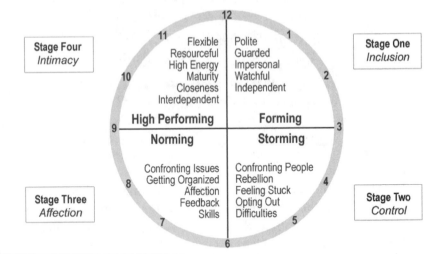

FORMING

Every stage is important and credible. During the first stage, Forming, team members come together and begin to learn about each other, to discover why they are part of a team, and to define their desired outcomes. Forming is represented on the team development clock between the hours of 12 and 3. Team leaders play an important role during this time—answering questions, providing direction, and building trust among team members. Team behaviors in the Forming stage are polite and guarded. Members are nice to each other, tend to avoid or delay conflicts, are hesitant to share their innermost secrets, strengths, and passions, and are watchful. On a personal level, the individual team member wonders about being included. Team members quietly ask themselves, "Will I be included in this team? What do I need for myself in order to feel like a real part of this team?"

Many teams become stuck in the Forming stage. This happens if membership is not stable, or if the team does not address differences of opinion, style, or outcomes. For some teams, the Forming stage may be sufficient. If the project or outcome is short-lived, all the work of the team can be accomplished in the Forming stage. For example, Andrea's neighbors came together to decide the process for purchasing and installing a fire hydrant. Tom completed research about what the fire department required, Bill took the action to find a hydrant for sale, and everyone agreed to split the costs evenly— easy, simple, complete. In our complex work environments, however, teams seldom have the luxury of staying in the comfort of Forming, because the tasks require ongoing relationships and increasingly complex performance.

Typical behaviors in the Forming stage include:

♠ Excitement.

♠ Apprehension.

♠ People are unclear about what their goals are as a team.

♠ Team members talk in terms of "I" instead of "we."

Storming

For a team to reach high performance, it must pass through Storming. Storming is uncomfortable for most people, and many will want to whiz right through this stage. Storming is represented on the team development clock between the hours of 3 and 6. All team members should know about Storming in advance, to reduce their apprehension and discomfort.

Disillusionment, frustration, and even anger are signs that Storming has begun. Members may begin to confront and experience irritation with each other. Members feel stuck. They may want to opt out of the team and its responsibilities, or rebel against the team or its leader. Decisions don't come easily. Cliques may form, and there will be power struggles.

It is a natural stage of evolution to move to Storming. Storming is like when a child advances to the Terrible Twos as a toddler. It's good news developmentally, but that doesn't mean it's fun! The individual issue that invariably emerges for a team in Storming is one of control. "How much control, power, and influence will I have in this group? How much do I want? How do I earn respect?"

The team leader at the Storming stage encounters *the* most important challenge he or she will face in guiding the development of the team—building the team's capacity to storm. As leader, you need to make it safe for team members to express differences of opinion, to disagree, listen, and reach new conclusions. You may be in the position of knowing there is unspoken or unresolved conflict on the team. This is what you *want* at this stage! When you encourage the expression of differences, and facilitate processes to resolve them, you build the team. You may very well have to push the team into Storming if they resist it, because Storming builds a very important skill for the rest of the team's life—the ability to manage conflict effectively. A successful experience with Storming builds confidence and reduces fear the next time a team faces a storm. When a team successfully navigates the storm, they bond, build trust and respect, and arrive at better decisions.

Donald, one of our clients, is an HR Director in a high-tech company, and he encountered the perfect storm in one day! Individually, four members of his team dropped by his office to complain about how someone else on the team was approaching salary planning, and how he or she thought it should go. Donald saw in a flash that his team was ready to storm. He called them together and assigned them their goal: to create a common process for salary planning for the entire division. Donald then left. Three hours later they emerged from the conference room with a process they all supported. The "esprit de corps" was palpable. They joked with each other, and began a period of true high performance. As a team leader, you may not be able to leave the room—Donald's people were very sophisticated in managing interpersonal relationships, and Donald encouraged each of them to be open and honest. However you do it, you must ensure the team storms, building the foundation for the next stage of development.

Typical behaviors in the Storming stage include:

♠ People feel "stuck."

♠ Some team members opt out of meetings, conversations, and conflicts.

♠ Team members complain about working together.

♠ People confront each other instead of the issues.

♠ There may be ideas, but few are explored in-depth.

♠ The tasks seem more difficult than anyone originally thought.

NORMING

Once a team has successfully navigated the hurricane, wild fire, or other crisis, it moves into the third stage: Norming. Norms are the accepted standards, ways of behaving, or methods for doing things. Norming is represented on the team development clock between the hours of 6 and 9, though the process of Norming exists throughout the entire team process. At some level, norms are continuously being created, reinforced, and broken. Team members articulate norms in creating ground rules during the Forming stage. In the Norming stage, the team revisits those norms and sets rules that more clearly reflect the unique operating style of this team. You will find guidelines for creating team ground rules—and other important team processes—in the Implementation Ideas section at the end of this chapter and on our Website.

You will know the team has entered Norming when topics (both inside and outside the team meeting) change from confronting people to confronting issues and barriers that impede achievement

193

of team objectives. Having learned that they will be included in the team and can use their ability to influence, members now have the self-confidence, safety, and security to open up to and respect each other. Real affection happens at this stage.

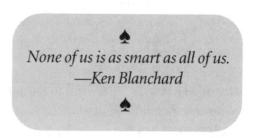

♠

None of us is as smart as all of us.
—Ken Blanchard

♠

Team members develop the skill and the commitment to provide honest feedback. The team organizes itself for maximum effectiveness, and engages a broad range of strengths from its members. Roles and responsibilities are clear and accepted. Commitment and unity are strong. What a team!

Typical behaviors in the Norming stage include:

- ♠ Team members provide each other with useful feedback.
- ♠ The team is organized, and able to make and monitor progress.
- ♠ Team members interact well—even bond.
- ♠ There is a mutual and shared understanding of the goals.

PERFORMING

Performing is represented on the team development clock between the hours of 9 and 12. Because the team is performing at some level throughout all the stages, we prefer to call this stage "High Performing." At the (High) Performing stage, the team is a well-oiled machine. Members are open, flexible, resourceful, and exhibit high energy. There is closeness and an unconscious process of working together, something magnificent to witness—even if you are outside the team. Emotional intimacy emerges in this stage, with team members immersed in what may be some of the most important and deep relationships of their work careers. The team knows clearly why it is doing what it is doing, and is able to stand on its own feet with no interference from the leader. The team works toward achieving goals, and also attends to relationship, style, and process issues along the way. If your team makes it this far, the rewards to the individual, the team, and the organization will be enormous!

It takes a *long* time for teams to reach the Performing stage. Two years is not unusual, though you will see glimpses of high performance along the way. Andrea considers herself privileged by twice being on a team that reached this stage, once as a member, and once as team leader. Both teams met frequently and had many interdependencies, and it still took 18–24 months to achieve *consistent* high performance. Once arrived, however, each team not only performed magnificently, but formed friendships that are still alive today.

Typical behaviors in the Performing stage include:

- ♠ Team members are highly resourceful.
- ♠ Team members support each other and the team.
- ♠ The team is highly successful at achieving its goals.
- ♠ It is fun to work in this team.
- ♠ The team creatively resolves problems.

AFTER THE PERFORMANCE

In Tuckman's new stage of Adjourning, the team completes the work and disengages from the task and the other team members. The team might also begin again—at midnight on the team-development clock—and start with a new charter. When you successfully navigate the waters of team leadership, and bring forth the best strengths from all team members, you have achieved a significant breakthrough that leaves you with a sense of remarkable accomplishment!

Trust

As a team forms and begins to move through the various stages of development, trust is a necessity. To illustrate, look at the following scenarios.

- ♠ Sydney told Emma she did a great job explaining the proposal to the client this morning. Emma knows Sydney is telling her the truth, because Sydney also tells her clearly and directly when she makes a mistake or does less than her best.

- ♠ Though Joe stated openly that his team messed up in the first phase of the project, the team remained enthusiastic, motivated, and engaged.

- ♠ Stan is having trouble with his young son, and he is coming to work late and leaving early. His colleagues, who rely heavily on Stan's work, are picking up the slack without a grumble.

- ♠ The purchasing department needed to layoff two people to meet corporate cost reductions. The department came together and made the decision who to let go.

What do all of the scenarios have in common? In each of these situations, the team has engendered trust. Trust is required for building relationships, tapping strengths, increasing productivity, and engaging workers. As you can see from Tuckman's model, trust is imperative for the team from the beginning. Building trust is ongoing and constant. It doesn't happen only at off-site team-building events; it happens every day. As the leader of a forming team, the way you speak about the strengths of each team member, the team purpose, and your vision of a great team all build trust. More important are your actions. "Walking your talk" through accountability, openness, curiosity, and commitment to the team builds trust faster than words.

Trust is the foundation—the infrastructure—of excellent relationships at work, at home, and in our broader lives. We don't give much thought to the infrastructure in our community until something goes wrong. Most of us don't pay attention to how many snowplows our town operates until the big 100-year snowstorm hits. We don't worry about the sewer backing up into our basement until the floods come.

Trust is similar. We don't consciously think about trust until a storm of words or actions destroys it. How often do we stop and consider what we are doing to build trust? When do we actually ask ourselves, "Am I consistently following through with the tasks that I'm assigned? Am I sharing information with colleagues to keep them informed and up-to-date on my responsibilities that affect them? Am I soliciting input from others so that I am acting on the best information?" Normally, we think about building trust only when it has been violated and desperately needs repair. As leaders, we can—and should—build trust constantly. It would serve us well to think about and begin building trust *before* trust is lost. Unfortunately, trust is often lost in a flash. A comment, question, or single incident can destroy fragile or shallow trust. Even more unfortunate, it takes much longer to rebuild trust than to create it in the first place.

If you create trust in a relationship, you will be able to enjoy cooperation, communication, and collaboration. Trust enhances your ability to influence and motivate others. Trust creates satisfying relationships. Trust builds strong teams.

BEHAVIORS THAT BUILD TRUST

So, what can you do today to increase trust on your team? The behaviors of trust are really quite simple to explain…though not always simple to do!

When we meet someone, we naturally want to trust the other person, and be trusted in return. However, if we don't quickly begin to build it, the opportunity for trust will dissipate. *The first rule of trust is to trust.* Assume each team member wants what is best for the team, and eagerly hopes to be able to bring his strengths, skills, and passions to bear. To build trust further, include these actions consciously and consistently:

Truthfulness

Respect

Understanding

Support

Time

TRUTHFULNESS

- ♠ Express emotions—how you feel—as well as facts.
- ♠ Walk your talk by taking actions congruent with what you say.
- ♠ Avoid excuses—tell the truth, even when it hurts.
- ♠ Provide feedback without judgment.
- ♠ Disclose information about yourself; take personal risks.

RESPECT

- ♠ Accept others as they are, without judgment. You don't need to control, fix, or change them. Remember, they are creative, resourceful, whole, and wise.
- ♠ Play to each other's strengths.

♠ Solicit ideas, opinions, and personal feedback from others.

♠ Listen when another person speaks.

♠ Maintain confidential information.

♠ Assign no blame.

♠ Respect different points of view—yours and others.

♠ Gain others' insights before making decisions affecting them.

♠ Repair relationships—don't avoid the conversation because you are uncomfortable.

UNDERSTANDING

♠ Learn more about one another's strengths, skills, and experiences. Team members need to know that each other is competent before they trust fully.

♠ Listen for the feelings underlying the words of the speaker.

SUPPORT

♠ Offer skills and resources; give help when needed.

♠ Build each other's confidence.

♠ Ask for help when you need it.

♠ Advocate for each person, and the team as a whole.

♠ Allow each other to share problems without judgment.

TIME

♠ Spend quality time in relationships.

♠ Spend quality time in dialogue.

♠ Be silent—give others time to think or express their thoughts.

♠ Be there in a time of need.

♠ Value and respect each other's time.

A Path for the Team

ACTIONS TO FACILITATE FORMING

You know about the stages of team development and how to build trust. You've studied the work that your staff needs to accomplish, and you've determined that success really does require "a small group of people with complementary skills committed to a common purpose, set of specific performance goals and an approach for which they hold themselves mutually accountable." So you decide to create a team. What steps do you take? Where do you begin? Let's explore the answers to these questions through Michael's good example at B2B Printers.

Michael decided to transform his staff into a bona fide team. The first stumbling block he encountered is the same one you're probably thinking about right now—you don't have the luxury of starting a team from scratch, with members who are brand new and eager! How can you begin at Forming? You have a group that has been performing, more or less effectively, as a team. It may be stuck at Storming, you may see glimpses of brilliant High Performance, it may be divisive or unified. It may be in all of these stages at different times!

Michael started with a few foundational actions. No matter at what stage your team is functioning, you always can cycle back to these Forming and Storming activities and build a stronger infrastructure with the team. Michael (wisely!) chose three actions to begin what he called *re*-Forming. He led his team to create a charter, establish ground rules, and identify and apply strengths in a one-day offsite meeting. Whether starting or restarting a new team, these actions facilitate Forming.

STEP 1. CREATE A CHARTER

For a team to form and unify, its members should create a team purpose, vision, and goals—a team charter. You might use the word *mission* instead of *purpose* or *desired state* instead of *vision*. It doesn't matter. What matters is that you and the team define the reason for your existence, the end state you desire, and the milestones that get you there.

The first order of business is to establish a purpose that answers the question, "why do we exist as a team?" Michael's sales managers chose this purpose: "As sales managers, we come together as a team to drive revenue strategically, to create visibility and opportunities for our sales associates, to create a unified face of B2B Printers to our customers, and to maximize the effectiveness and accuracy of our sales process." Motivating, isn't it?!

When a team can clearly identify what it intends to accomplish, it naturally leads into vision, the second component of the team charter. The vision is the inspiration behind the purpose. Vision is the dream—what's possible, or maybe even a little bit impossible.

It's a compelling image of the team purpose accomplished, the ideal future state. When guided by a vision, people believe their efforts can make a difference, and they'll work with greater commitment.

An inspiring vision:

- ♠ depicts future achievements.
- ♠ invokes a vivid picture.
- ♠ suggests a measure for high performance.
- ♠ speaks to the common values of the team.
- ♠ prompts integration and collaboration.

When I dare to be powerful, to use my strength in the service of my vision, then it becomes less and less important whether I am afraid.
—Audre Lorde

Michael's team developed a vision that paints a vivid picture of their future success: "A waiting list of excellent people want to join the Western Division of B2B Printers because we develop employees, consistently grow revenue, and totally delight customers."

With inspiration from this compelling vision, the team dove into its third and final task in creating its charter: setting team goals. Through lively discussion, they created the following package of high-level goals. They were prepared to measure their progress and hold themselves mutually accountable to:

- ♠ Charter a team to design and implement an effective leads process by June 30; "effective" to be defined by the team and approved by the sponsor, Keith; target date for implementation to be determined.

- ♠ By September 30, commit to a process to gather information about development needs and opportunities for sales associates. By December 31, be prepared to charter the next step.

- ♠ Hold a "Sales Synergies" conference in September to explore ways to exploit the western territory by industry, common business processes, and/or geography.

- ♠ Take the actions necessary to form, storm (yuck!), norm, and highly perform! Undertake a specific task or action at each weekly staff meeting to move us in this direction. Michael is accountable to create a plan by June 1.

Michael knew that establishing accountability—for individuals and the team as a whole—was a critical part of the charter. With *individual accountability,* team members take full responsibility to complete their own assignments. *Interlocking accountability* occurs when team members take ownership for their own conduct and also their obligations to others, creating an environment in which people can count on each other. Michael facilitated the team, establishing interlocking accountability tied to the team's goals. Each team member agreed that he was not only responsible for assignments, but also for his relationships, his performance, his agreements, for holding other team members accountable, and for *all* of the team's goals. They all knew team success was a priority over individual success, and that the whole was truly greater than the sum of the parts.

That was a day well spent! The team emerged from its meeting even more engaged, committed, and enthusiastic about future potential. Now, ever vigilant about applying his strengths, Michael reviewed the day and noticed how effectively he used his strengths to lead the team through these activities. He revisited his strengths:

♠ Initiating: I turn thoughts into action.

♠ Developing others: I develop others, *especially* their strengths!

♠ Influencing: I win others over.

♠ Learning: I acquire knowledge and learn fast.

♠ Amplifying: I transform something (or someone!) from good to great.

He acknowledged that he used his strengths of initiating and developing others. He also saw that he applied his influencing strength when he could have been using his learning strength. In reviewing the conversations of the day, he realized that he might have been advocating for his position a little too often, instead of drawing others out. Well, there's still much to work on! Best of all, though, he knew that he was turning his staff into a strong team. Ah, the beauty of playing his best cards!

STEP 2. ESTABLISH GROUND RULES

We each enter a new team with different assumptions about what makes for ideal interactions. To build a strong team, be clear from the beginning how members work with one another. At the earliest stages of team formation, members need to define specific attitudes and actions that are their standards for interacting. Create team ground rules to guide the team members in how to operate effectively as a team and achieve its purpose.

In organizations, real power and energy is generated through relationships. The patterns of relationships and the capacities to form them are more important than tasks, functions, roles, and positions.
—Margaret Wheatley

This is precisely what Michael did next—create team behavioral agreements. (One of our favorite methods for creating team ground rules is at the end of this chapter in *Implementation Ideas.*)

Here's what Michael's team agreed to:

♠ Check egos, titles, positions, and other judgments, labels, and "baggage" at the door.

♠ Act in the spirit of collaboration, not contention. Maintain a "solution-oriented" frame of mind (no blaming, shaming, bashing, whining, complaining, pouting, withdrawing, or rehashing history).

♠ State your point of view clearly, once, and offer data or rationale to back it up.

♠ Be respectful of each person expressing a point of view and allow each person to speak uninterrupted. Listen thoughtfully and consider with an open mind the opinions of others.

♠ Come to team meetings prepared to participate as a fully engaged team member. Accept responsibility and ownership for team goals, accountabilities, strengths, and weaknesses.

♠ Use feedback as a growth and learning opportunity. Offer it to others respectfully and constructively, and be open-minded to receiving it in the spirit of learning.

♠ Complete our commitments—or renegotiate as early as possible.

♠ Play to our strengths!

♠ Have fun!

Further, Michael's team agreed to post their ground rules in their offices and regular meeting rooms, as well as to use them at their annual strategy meeting.

STEP 3. IDENTIFY AND APPRECIATE DIVERSE STRENGTHS

The third action Michael chose was to increase team appreciation of differences. He knows this is important for building team trust and reliance upon one another, to encourage different perspectives and ideas, and to facilitate better team decisions.

At the time, team members had already completed the Clifton StrengthsFinder assessment, identifying their individual strengths. Michael created a matrix of team member strengths, and, together, they explored team patterns of strengths and the implications for team members. He knows that on high-performance teams, people say they call upon their strengths more than 75 percent of the time.[3] Thus, it's critical for team members to know each other's strengths, so they can play to and maximize them.

Next, seeking another reference point, Michael invited a facilitator to administer and interpret the Myers-Briggs Type Inventory (MBTI), which gave team members helpful information about each other's preferred styles in gathering information, making decisions, and communicating. The MBTI instrument, extremely popular in organizations of all kinds across the world, requires a qualified facilitator.

Whew! We've just described the three steps Michael took to transform his group of sales associates at B2B Printers into a fully formed team. As his team progresses through the team development stages, he will want to use specific methods and focused activities to help it evolve and progress. We invite you to visit our Website—*www.play2yourstrengths.com*—for additional insights and activities for the Forming, Storming, Norming, and Performing steps of team development.

Improving Team Communication

Throughout its stages of development, a team requires many additional skills—effective communication among them.

Daily discussions in meetings, conversations in the hallways, decision-making, and interactions with coworkers and other teams require team members to advocate, clarify, summarize, acknowledge, listen, and speak nondefensively. The two most important communication skills for the team are advocacy and inquiry.

The crucial role of language in human evolution was not the ability to exchange ideas, but the increased ability to cooperate.
—*Fritjof Capra*

Advocacy

Dictionary.com defines advocacy as "active support of an idea or cause." Simply stated, it's the ability to offer one's point of view. Sounds easy enough, right? Yes and no. To advocate effectively takes skill. Have you ever been in a conversation with someone who has *very* strong verbal skills? Occasionally that individual may have a tendency to advocate, advocate, advocate! Advocacy is not about bullying or wearing people down until they agree with you. It's actually about engaging the other person in a dialogue, and inviting their curiosity. Some powerful tactics for sound advocacy are:

- ♠ Share your perspective and its rationale, disclosing not only your thinking, but also your assumptions. "Here's my viewpoint on this issue and how I got there..."

- ♠ Invite others to react to your view and challenge your assumptions. "What do you think?"

- ♠ Encourage them to provide a different view or to challenge yours. How do you see it differently? What have I missed?"

Sometimes we simply share our point of view. Other times, when the stakes are high, we take a stand with fierceness for all the right reasons. To be in the right frame of mind for effective team communication, it is helpful to ask yourself, prior to advocating your point of view, "what is my intention in this conversation? Am I willing to be influenced?"

Inquiry

Inquiry is the "trump card" for inviting others into a dialogue with you. How can anyone resist answering a great question? Effective inquiry is not interrogation—it is *genuine* and *respectful* natural curiosity. Specific methods of inquiry that invite conversation include:

- ♠ Use open-ended coaching questions that encourage a more thorough answer than yes or no from the other person. "What does marketing need to know before we implement?"

♠ Ask for the other person's rationale, and how he arrived at that perspective, to discover what assumptions he is holding. "Help me understand your reasoning..."

Listening, too, is a natural part of inquiry—they are two sides of the same coin. After asking questions, engage your ears, eyes, body, and mind to really *hear* the other person. Habit number five in Stephen Covey's best-seller, *The 7 Habits of Highly Effective People*, states, "Seek first to understand, then to be understood." Rather than scheming to debate the other person's position or being distracted by the to-do list in your head, listen for new information; listen for common perspectives; and, based on genuine curiosity, listen to be enlightened by another point of view.

Uncover Team Strengths

We know the strengths of individual team members; we now can look at the strengths of the team as a whole—a *collective*. When you draw the fifth card to complete your Dolly Parton straight from 9-to-5, you transform your hand. Instead of a collection of cards, you have a hand that could win a pot! The whole is much greater than the sum of the parts. Similarly, once you know individuals' strengths on the team, you're ready to search for the *team* strengths.

Reminding one another of the dream that each of us aspires to may be enough for us to set each other free.
—Antoine de Saint-Exupéry

Appreciative Inquiry (AI) is a powerful and practical process to uncover team strengths. AI assumes that everyone has a core of strengths, and that positive change occurs by identifying—and then doing more of—what each individual, team, or organization does well. Sounds familiar, doesn't it? Appreciative Inquiry searches for the best in people, their organizations, and their world. AI is being used to identify team and organization strengths in such diverse entities as The University of Michigan, The Camp Recovery Center, Pfizer, Boeing, John Deere, and the U.S. Navy.

Appreciative Inquiry accomplishes two important things: it illuminates strengths, and it shows how to repeat, multiply, and magnify those strengths. Through AI, your team zeroes in on "what works great around here," and fosters a climate that creates opportunities to do more of that!

There are four primary steps to the Appreciative Inquiry process. However, there is a crucial "prework" task—creating the question(s) to open up the constructive dialogue about team strengths. There are innumerable variations, but the basic format resembles one or more of these inquiries:

- ♠ Describe a time when you or the team performed really well. What were the circumstances that made this possible?

- ♠ Describe a time during your career in this organization when you felt most effective and engaged. What circumstances made the situation possible?

- ♠ Talk about an incident when you or someone else on the team truly delighted a customer. What made that possible?

What we focus on, individually and collectively, prospers by our attention. We urge you to think carefully about how to ask the AI questions, highlighting "What we are doing right" to keep the discussion focused on strengths.

After you carefully craft the question or questions, you're ready to begin the AI conversation. See Implementation Ideas at the end of this chapter for instructions on facilitating this important dialogue.

When teams use the Appreciative Inquiry process, every member begins to work from a natural place of strength. The team begins to use previously neglected strengths, and they also become more deliberate about where their team strengths are serving them well—and where they need to invite in different strengths to represent missing concepts, ideas, and perspectives. As you empower more success and engagement through this process—more opportunities for the team to play to its strengths—you create geometrically more opportunities!

Coaching a Team to Strengths

Carol coached a team into their strengths when she was senior director of global leadership and learning with a Silicon Valley high-tech firm. Prior to Carol's arrival, the department experienced considerable turnover, the leadership direction was sketchy at best, and the rest of the organization viewed the department as an unproductive cost center that created products marginally helpful, but barely responsive to their needs. There was an incessant, frenzied push to throw products and programs out to internal customers without much thought for strategic direction, planning, customer inputs, or needs analysis.

The VP would swing back and forth in management style—from sheer neglect of staff members to micromanaging the most tedious project details. The pervading culture kept decision-making authority (both strategic and tactical) at the highest levels, not delegated to the more appropriate lower levels in the organizations. Managers were frustrated by having no input and no authority for decisions on projects.

Team members, in a state of fear and frustration, were confused about how and if their work was valued, how it contributed to the larger organization, what the true priorities were, how performance was measured, and the perceived inequities (especially during bonus time). Not surprisingly, deep morale issues pervaded this global 45-member team. They feared they wouldn't do what was expected, would be on the receiving end of the VP's unpredictable wrath, and would lose their jobs. They didn't know how to integrate their strengths into their work, and they didn't have the authority to do so.

Carol wasted no time in taking decisive actions to strengthen the team. She began by honoring the hard work, dedication, and talent that had led to successful projects in the past. Carol acknowledged each individual and his or her unique contribution, and celebrated the product successes of each project team.

She searched for the strengths of individuals, so she could acknowledge not just what they had accomplished, but also who they were being while accomplishing it. She looked for patterns of strengths used effectively.

Carol facilitated a shared vision for each project currently under way or on the radar screen—talking about the work's objectives and outcomes, how the project benefits customers, and how it fit in with the overall mission of the company.

She established an infrastructure to keep employees focused on their strengths, including weekly project team meetings and one-on-one coaching with all direct reports and project team leads.

She discussed strengths with each team member and adjusted project roles and responsibilities to ensure the work suited each team member's strengths and passions.

She clarified and articulated the strengths of the team, aligning and engaging them around a common purpose, and setting clear interlocking accountabilities.

The results? Engagement, dedication, and satisfaction rose, significantly increasing morale. The products, services, and reputation of the department improved dramatically, and they received positive feedback and praise from their client departments throughout the organization, even winning an industry award for their work.

Not a bad story, huh? You, too, can create a strong team by completing the Dolly Parton straight in your team, and playing that full, strong hand to everyone's advantage at work!

Dolly Parton—Completing the 9-to-5 Straight

We thought you'd appreciate this story from *The Cultural Creatives* by Paul H. Ray and Sherry Ruth Anderson. In the Arizona desert, there is a solar collector constructed of an immense array of freestanding mirrors. Every mirror reflects the sun's light onto a single collector tower that heats water to more than a thousand degrees, driving turbines for electricity. Each mirror is curved slightly and pivots independently under sensitive computer control to track the sun's beams and keep them focused on the tower. All of them together are the equivalent of a gigantic parabolic mirror.

The metaphor of this story illustrates the potent premise of this chapter: The power reflected by uncoordinated individual actions has little effect; however, focus 10 or a thousand individuals on the creative fire, and let them move independently, but with a common purpose, and magnificent focused energy materializes.

A ♣

Implementation Ideas

We include instructions for a number of processes in this section. Visit our Website for downloadable versions of all instructions.

BUY A GUMBY!

For Gumby fans, or those of us into nostalgia, Gumby is once again available at many stores! Here's a great place to begin looking: *www.toyscollectibles.allinfo-about.com/subjects/gumby.html*

STUDY AND APPLY TUCKMAN'S MODEL OF TEAM DEVELOPMENT

See *www.chimaeraconsulting.com/tuckman.htm* and *www.businessballs.com/tuckmanformingstormingnormingperforming.htm.*

CREATE A CHARTER

To successfully form and unify, a team should create a team purpose, vision, and goals. We suggest discussing:

- ♠ Why do we exist as a team?
- ♠ What can we attain that cannot be attained by operating as individuals or as a group? What synergies can we anticipate?
- ♠ What do we hope for? What is our vision?
- ♠ What are our significant team goals?

Here is an exercise to help your team create a vision. You may want to change the date and award to suit your organization.

It is July 31, 2013 (choose a date five or more years in the future), and your department has just been presented with the Fast Company Award for the "Most Innovative Product in the Industry." Imagine the editor hires you to write a 500- to 1,500-word article telling readers about your team's successes. Bring it with you to the team meeting on establishing the charter. Yes, you get to define "best." Be as tangible as you can. What has the team accomplished in the last five years? Who has it served, and how has it served them? What affect has it had on the people and the communities in which it works? What affect has it had on the world? How is this team unique? What is notable about the internal workings of the team—how is it managed? What is its culture? Who does the team partner with in its unique style of relating to its customers? What are the most pervasive strategies and tactics that have brought it such success in these five years? What's the next big milestone, after 2013, envisioned by the team?

Invite team members to read their articles. We once worked with a team at Novell that did this exercise first thing in the morning of their full-day retreat. They became so clear about their vision of what was possible, they stopped the meeting, and told us (the consultants) to go away—they didn't need us anymore. They prepared a presentation for the CEO, met with him before the day was out, and proceeded to create one of Novell's most successful products.

WRITE TEAM GROUND RULES

To create your team's ground rules or norms, try this process. It is a bit surprising that it begins with the challenge of defining typical behaviors in an *un*successful team. However, you'll find it smoothly transitions to identifying specific strategies and tactics that set up the team for success.

Step 1

In your team, answer the question, "what would we have to do to be a totally unsuccessful team?" Also, consider "what have we done in the past, in our interactions with each other, that wasn't productive?" Brainstorm and record the specific behaviors and actions that contribute to being a truly dysfunctional team. These aren't hard to come up with—we would dare say each of us has either (accidentally?) pulled these shenanigans, or been the victim of them, on more than one occasion. Examples:

- ♠ Discounting or shooting down ideas.
- ♠ Interrupting.
- ♠ Not participating fully in meetings.
- ♠ Coming late to meetings.
- ♠ Bad-mouthing team members.

Step 2

As a team, choose the three to five behaviors from your list that would cause the biggest problems for your group.

Step 3

Determine specific behaviors that will ensure your team effectively *avoids* these problems. Use strong and positive language to identify what team members *will* do. Instead of "we don't arrive late," try, "we arrive five minutes early."

Step 4

Ask each person on the team if these behaviors constitute the ground rules for interacting on this team. Ask each if they are willing to abide by these ground rules. Also, ask if they are willing to enforce them. Tweak the wording of any ground rule that doesn't feel right; make sure each is agreed upon and accepted by everyone. When the entire team is authorized and empowered to abide by and uphold the team ground rules, you have ground rules with teeth. Decide among yourselves how and when you call an infraction of the rules. Do we call a behavior in the moment? Do we interrupt to do so?

APPRECIATE DIVERSE INDIVIDUAL AND TEAM STRENGTHS

In addition to the Appreciative Inquiry process identified in this chapter, here's another great exercise for uncovering the collective strengths of your team:

♠ After all team members have completed the Clifton StrengthsFinder, Myers-Briggs Type Indicator, and other self-assessment instruments, bring members together and facilitate a rich, in-depth discussion of each team member's competencies.

♠ Ask the team to focus on the *collective* perspective: What are the strengths and competencies of this team? What are our successes, our failures? What do we love to do together? What are we passionate about? What is easy for us in our day-to-day work as a group?

♠ Refine, edit, and create a list of six to eight team strengths.

♠ Rate each strength on how well the team is leveraging it today.

♠ Create a table that lists the top five strengths of each member and the top-five strengths in the team as a whole.

♠ Discuss how the team can leverage these individual and team strengths even more.

The team strengths profiling exercise highlights the diversity and uniqueness of each team member, while allowing them to assign appropriate and meaningful responsibilities based upon strengths.

Conduct the Team Strengths Activity

Michael designed an activity to *ground* each team member in his strengths. He knows now that enabling team members to use their strengths improves team performance, and teamwork is at its best only when complementary strengths align. Because team members rely upon each other, it is best for the team to understand how to support each other using their strengths—and not their weaknesses. We thought you might like to see what Michael did. (This activity is adapted from Marcus Buckingham's *Go Put Your Strengths to Work*, Free Press, 2007) Each team member in turn engaged in this conversation with the team:

One of my strengths is _____, and here's how I think we could leverage it. What are your thoughts? How can you help me leverage my strength for the good of the team?

The speaker then put a key weakness on the table.

One of my weaknesses is _____. What ideas do you have for how I can spend less time using my weakness? How can you help me work around it?

Finally, the speaker restated one of his key strengths and asked each team member to relate one instance when the speaker demonstrated this strength.

This exercise builds confidence and competence in each member's strengths, amplifies the team's focus on individual and collective strengths, and strengthens the bonds of support and integration among its individual members.

FACILITATE THE APPRECIATIVE INQUIRY PROCESS

The prework component of AI is to create the question(s) that will open up the constructive dialogue about team strengths. Here are three examples of questions to get the team started:

- ♠ Describe a time when you or the team performed really well. What were the circumstances that made this possible?

- ♠ Describe a time during your career in this organization when you felt most effective and engaged. What circumstances made the situation possible?

- ♠ Talk about an incident when you or someone else on the team truly delighted a customer. What made that possible?

Tweak the question so that it is most pertinent to your organization. Think carefully about how to frame it, highlighting "what we are doing right" to keep the discussion focused on strengths.

Decide whom to invite into the AI conversation. It could be just you and the team, or you could invite some customers! You can start big or small. Allow ample time (three to four hours or more), to engage fully with the question. Work through these four steps of AI:

Step 1: Discovery

Discovery is about appreciating the best. This is where you ask your well-crafted questions. Seek, discover, appreciate, and value those points of strength, where your team did what they do well. Participants typically experience high energy and positivism. Encourage full participation by using small groups if needed to ensure everyone's engagement. Have each group share the most exciting information they uncovered. You'll create a powerful shift in the room that everyone will experience.

Step 2: Dream

In this next step, envision what could happen if you (the team) create the circumstances to support doing more of what works well. What results/impact can you expect if you set yourselves up to play to these team strengths? Notice how this idea is fully grounded in reality and past experience. It's a different process altogether from typical vision because it creates inspiring answers to what might be possible if you pave the way to repeat and sustain such excellence in team strength.

Step 3: Design

In step three of AI, talk about how to change your processes to create opportunities for repeating your successes. How do you need to reconstruct your work so that you ensure more of these delightful, high-performance experiences? What barriers do you need to tear down? What supporting mechanisms can you build?

Step 4: Destiny

This final step is one of innovating and committing. What will you (the team) do to fertilize your strength opportunities? What actions do you choose to take? And when will you conduct an appreciative inquiry session again? It's an intuitive/iterative process that builds on itself.

GET COMFORTABLE WITH CONFLICT AND POWER

Conflict happens, especially during the Storming stage of team development. *Handling Conflict,* provided by CRM Films (*www.crmlearning.com*), can help us understand our preferences for dealing with conflict. Also from CRM Films, rent *The Abilene Paradox* and its facilitator's guide to explore the fascinating topic of Groupthink.

The Thomas-Kilmann Conflict Mode Instrument is a great resource for understanding our preferred conflict styles. You can purchase it at *www.cpp.com*.

Because there is a profound link between power and conflict, you might enjoy reading the "Sources of Power" article by Andrea on our Website, *www.play2yourstrengths.com*.

ESTABLISH TEAM ACCOUNTABILITY

The attitude of team accountability holds that team success is more important than the success of individuals. The whole is greater than the sum of the parts. How do we accomplish that? Steps we have found helpful for creating team accountability include:

- ♠ Review the team charter, including purpose, vision, and goals. Ensure that each person feels responsible for the success of the team by linking the team's charter with team and individual actions.

- ♠ Create action plans for accomplishing a vision and assign responsibility for all actions.

- ♠ Challenge team members to hold each other accountable with acknowledgement and support, building safety for the team.

- ♠ Make thought diversity the norm. Solicit multiple points of view for decision-making and problem-solving.

- ♠ Encourage skeptics and doubters. Create a culture that welcomes challenges and "push back," in which important questions such as "Why?" and "Why not?"

219

are readily asked and answered without defensiveness.

♠ Monitor and measure the team's performance.

♠ Support mistakes and errors—embrace them as opportunities to learn and improve.

IMPROVE TEAM COMMUNICATION

Teach your team members about the important communication skills of advocacy, inquiry, and listening. Encourage members to become adept at using these skills in all of their interactions at work (and in life!). (See our Website for additional resources on the skills of communication, and other tools for teams.)

Read the "Enable Drumbeat Communications" article by Andrea on our Website to discover a method for devising a strategic communication plan within your team.

WATCH A GOOD MOVIE

Watch *Oceans Eleven* for an entertaining perspective on the importance of individual and team strengths! You may also want to rent *Nine to Five* for a comic view on how *not* to lead!

LEARN THE MBTI

A resource for the Myers-Briggs Type Indicator (MBTI) is available at *www.cpp.com*. You need a qualified facilitator to administer and interpret the MBTI with your team. Visit our Website to gain access to the Myers-Briggs Type Indicator.

READ A GOOD BOOK

Try these for good reading:

Discovering the Leader in You by Robert Lee and Sara King, published by Jossey-Bass and the Center for Creative Leadership, 2001.

The Wisdom of Teams: Creating the High Performance Organization by Jon R. Katzenbach and Douglas K. Smith, Collins, 2003.

The Cultural Creatives: How 50 Million People Are Changing the World by Paul Ray and Sherry Ruth Anderson, Harmony Books, 2000.

The Oz Principle: Getting Results Through Individual and Organizational Accountability Roger Connors, Tom Smith, and Craig Hickman, Portfolio Hardcover, 2004.

Navigating Change: A Field Guide to Personal Growth by Gary Gore, Team Trek, 2002.

Chapter Eight
Go All In:
Committing the
Full House

Go all in: To bet all of one's money.

In the wildly popular Discovery Channel program *Dirty Jobs*, producer and host Mike Rowe has found his true calling—traveling the United States in search of the dirtiest and smelliest jobs, and paying tribute to the unsung heroes who hold them. He apprentices under these experts and digs deep into the muck and filth to uncover the true value of each unique role. Rowe is perfect for this unusual show; he is personable, laughs easily, is anxious to learn, and eager to gain new perspectives that break old stereotypes. On the Discovery Channel Webpage, Rowe says, "Fun and hard work are two sides of the same coin," and he claims to value sacrifice, good humor, and optimism. Well-known entertainment personalities say Rowe is all of this in real life—not just on camera. He's compassionate, down-to-earth, and loves learning—and he has boosted *Dirty Jobs* to the number-1 position in Discovery Channel's lineup. Calling on his strengths and passions, Rowe takes on the worst work in the world and generates personal pride from a job well done!

What if every person in your organization performed a job (dirty or clean) that was a perfect match with his or her unique strengths?

223

Imagine what would happen to productivity and excellence in the organization. We know a janitor in a hospital who excels in all he does. Here's what he says about his work: "I'm the janitor here, and the best janitor anywhere in any hospital. Our doctors, nurses, and visitors expect a clean hospital. Our patients need it to be clean. That's what I give them."

This chapter is for senior leaders responsible for the culture and systems of their organizations, human resource professionals at every level, and managers who want their influence to be felt organization-wide. We look at the levers you pull to create a strengths-based culture. We take a strategic view of how strengths, as a framework, can be infused in organizations, by peering into the organization's *people systems* and its *culture*. When you "go all in" you hold nothing back. You have such a strong hand that you put everything on the table (literally!). Your "full house" is all your organizational systems working in concert to maximize the organization's strengths. You already know that fewer than one out of five employees play to his strengths every day at work. There are ways to increase this percentage in your organization, perhaps to an astounding 100 percent!

Senior leaders must be the champions for such an effort, because they carry the responsibility and the power to build the most effective organization they can. If they have not profiled their organization for strengths, they have considerable untapped potential. Strengths are the key to unlocking it. As we saw in Chapter 7♠, the whole is greater than the sum of the parts when we use the strengths of individuals on a team and the strengths of the team overall. Multiply this effect by all the teams in your organization and just imagine the possibilities!

A 2001 study involving 160 hospitals compared a group of employees who completed various strengths-based interventions throughout a three-year period, with a control group that did not have strengths-based activities. The hospitals using strengths development interventions grew significantly in employee engagement throughout three years, as compared to the control group.[1]

The effective executive builds on strengths—their own strengths, the strengths of superiors, colleagues, subordinates, and on the strength of the situation.
—Peter Drucker

A study conducted in 2002 in the automobile industry generated similar data. Another study across 65 companies in manufacturing, retail, healthcare, and technology industries reproduced these results. One analysis showed that the difference in employee engagement as a result of utilizing strengths amounts to $1,000 in additional productivity per employee.[2] It strikes us that $1,000, while significant, is really quite low—especially for knowledge workers and leaders, who influence and affect so many people. Either way, there's great potential when you make strategic, strengths-based shifts in systems and processes in your organization!

Job, Career, or Calling?

An office cleaner completes her work for the evening, noticing with satisfaction that the wastebaskets are empty, the floor vacuumed, and empty coffee cups gone. She leaves, pleased with her night's work. Her colleague, working two floors up, takes a slightly different perspective. When she leaves 15 minutes later, the coffee cups and wastebaskets are clean and the floor vacuumed. However, she has also watered the plants of workers on vacation, put fresh water in cut flower arrangements, and rescued thrown-away plants, nursing them back to life and then putting them back on window ledges. Eventually, her manager notices her additional work, which is not in her job description. How her manager reacts to this extra work and commitment will determine if this woman continues to stay engaged and enthusiastic about her role—or if she cuts back and does only what is required of her.

In *Positive Organizational Scholarship* (Berrett, 2003), Amy Wrzesniewski writes about three orientations toward work. People who view work as a *job* focus on the material rewards of work, and not on meaning and fulfillment. They see their jobs as the means to providing enjoyment in areas outside of work, such as interests and hobbies. People with a *career*-orientation work for the increased pay, prestige, and status that comes through promotions and advancement. Advancement brings with it increased self-esteem, power, and social standing. Those with the third orientation, viewing their work as a *calling*, work for fulfillment. The work is an end to itself, along with the belief that their work makes the world a better place.[3]

While we might want all of our employees to see their work as a *calling*, that's not realistic. These work orientations are not controlled by organizational practices or by the job itself, but by the individual in the job. In fact, in a study of job orientations, 24 administrative assistants were evenly divided, eight in each of the three orientations. Similar job descriptions supported all three orientations, though those with a *calling* orientation—here and in another study of 425 employees—reported higher job satisfaction, more commitment to their work teams, and more faith and trust in management.[4]

What if we, as leaders in organizations, created systems that nurtured all three orientations? What if, regardless of employee orientation, the work in your organization exactly met the desires, needs, and strengths of each employee? This is possible if we change organizational systems to focus on strengths and align individuals' strengths and passions with their work. By leveraging its people systems and by directly influencing the culture, an organization will naturally begin to use its strengths in a bigger way. Systems and culture are the levers—and as leaders, we control them.

PEOPLE SYSTEMS

A few people systems are particularly relevant to building a strengths-based culture: systems that attract, acquire, and onboard employees; systems that manage performance; systems that develop capability; and the most powerful "people" system: leadership.

Systems That Attract, Acquire, and Onboard

JOB DESIGN

Flexible job design is the first system to maximize opportunities for employees to engage strengths. If, as with our office cleaner, the job can be flexible enough to allow her time, space, and even resources to integrate her passion for plants into her work, then the job may maximize her strengths. While job descriptions outline the work to be performed and the outcomes to be achieved, how can we tweak them to encourage more worker flexibility? You know how most job descriptions end with the final bullet: "Other duties as assigned?" What if that final bullet read, "Other responsibilities as determined by the worker's to provide higher levels of customer delight than outlined above?"

ROLES

It's more than just the job description, of course, that drives flexibility in the work itself. If leaders view themselves as partners with employees, if they enable employees to work in a way that uses their strengths, they can build more flexibility into roles, inviting employees to craft their ideal jobs. Whether I view my role as a job, a career, or a calling, I could design what I do and how I do it, so that my job makes the best use of the talents I have to offer.

HIRING

As we discussed in Chapter 5♠, attracting and acquiring employees can certainly be built on a foundation of strengths. Job postings can list crucial strengths that the ideal candidate would possess. Seeking skills *and* strengths raises the quality of new hires.

Managers can learn to interview for strengths. When they hear the candidate claim a skill or competency, they can probe with, "What is the talent or strength you possess that underlies your skill? How do you know you possess that strength?" Other useful questions to interview for strengths are, "At what do you naturally excel? What is easy for you? What do you enjoy? What are you passionate about? Tell me about a time when you were highly successful at..."

EXTERNAL RELATIONSHIPS

Because we're talking about hiring, consider also your network of external contractors, vendors, suppliers, and consultants. What are the criteria you use today to hire from the temporary and flexible workforce? We purchase expertise when we hire external Website designers or computer engineers for specific skills we don't possess. How might you use these resources to manage the weaknesses of your employees?

For example, many professionals with limited administrative and computer expertise spend untold well-compensated hours building their PowerPoint presentations or making travel arrangements. In a strengths-based organization, people with the right strengths to excel at these tasks complete them, not a leader who is serving other needs—needs better aligned with her strengths. If we understand both the strengths and the weaknesses of the organization and its employees, might we allocate resources differently? Off-loading work to the right people with the right strengths makes it easier for employees to concentrate on work that utilizes their own strengths.

ONBOARDING

If we are attracting and acquiring employees for their strengths, and not just for their skills and experience, we invite a level of uniqueness into how each person performs her job. The onboarding process should also leverage this uniqueness. Remember in Chapter 6♠ when Michael custom-tailored Anna's onboarding at B2B Printers so that she could excel in using her strengths right from the start? An organization can endorse this practice for *all* managers. Tweak any

228

onboarding process documentation that exists, and explicitly state the organization's commitment to identifying and using strengths when you deliver new employee orientation programs. Affirm and confirm—in as many ways as possible—that your organization is truly interested in every individual identifying and applying her strengths at work.

Systems That Manage Performance

PERFORMANCE PLANNING

To build a strengths-based organization, existing performance planning and review processes may also require changes. If your organization already has an effective process that creates performance goals between the manager and the employee, you're on the right path! In a strengths-based culture, performance planning will also include a discussion about the opportunities the employee will have to apply her strengths. Such a focus increases commitment to achieving goals, because the employee better understands how to utilize her natural gifts.

Business-as-usual assessment has been tilted—understandably— toward identifying weaknesses, deficiencies, and problems. The positive psychology perspective expands (not replaces) traditional assessment to include areas of strengh and competence.
—Christopher Peterson, Ph.D.

PERFORMANCE ASSESSMENT

More and more organizations are developing competency models for specific roles—for leaders, for customer service representatives, sometimes for the entire company. Competency models spell out what performance the organization desires and expects. A good model includes behavioral anchors that describe excellent, average, and poor performance in each competency. We have an opportunity to mine these models for strengths.

An excellent model identifies what strengths underpin performance for each competency. Unfortunately, we tend to consider these models through the lens of, "Where do we need to improve? "What if we first explore Where do we excel, and how can we do more of that?" When we make this shift, we'll begin to utilize the full power and scope of the competency model!

REWARD SYSTEMS

Assessing and rewarding performance in a strengths-based culture calls forth the best coaching skills of your organization's managers and leaders. A powerful motivational practice is to "catch people doing things right." In a strengths-based organization, the trick is not only to catch them doing it right, but also to acknowledge the demonstrated strength, noting who the employee is *being* when she is *doing* what she does so well.

To illustrate, imagine your employee Bob is very creative. When Bob facilitates an innovative solution to a problem, a good manager knows to thank and acknowledge him for the great solution. Looking through the lens of strengths, you would also acknowledge Bob's innate creativity that led to the solution. This builds his confidence and competence in this strength, and helps Bob see how he applied it in this instance. Of course, the next step with Bob is to seek out other opportunities crying for his creativity!

Organizations' typical reward and recognition practices tend to focus on specific goal or task accomplishment. This, of course, is still important! However, we would like to see organizations add a criterion into the process—one that rewards specifically for applying a strength. In addition to the rewards that accrue to the team that designed an innovative solution, a performance reward can also be given to Bob for his excellent use of creativity.

This isn't as far-fetched as it sounds. Many excellent organizations with well-developed reward processes have recognition events to acknowledge corporate values in action, such as demonstrating "teamwork" or "flexibility." Creating awards for a consistent, excellent application of strength is a small, but effective, addition to the reward and recognition process, and reinforces the organization's continued commitment to strengths while highlighting the shift to a strengths-based organization.

Systems That Develop Capability

DEVELOPMENT PLANNING

People-development systems are the primary lever for increasing an organization's competence in managing and building strengths. An easy system to change is development planning. In Chapter 4♠ we gave you a sample of a strengths development template we use with many of our clients. (You can also find it on our Website.) In addition to setting specific performance goals, employees also set strength development goals. This simple yet sweeping change can begin to alter the conversation between employees and their managers.

When you make such a change in the development process, you also have to equip the leaders for important discussions with their employees about strength development. Our client, Maggie, vice president of learning in a hospital system, first equipped the hospitals' leaders with strengths knowledge and understanding before encouraging employees to discuss strengths with their boss. Every leader engaged in a process to discover her strengths, and received individualized coaching to further clarify them; she wrote her own strength development plan before she began to coach others on their strengths. This cost the hospital a little more than simply changing the development planning form; however, relatively quickly, "strengths" conversations could be heard throughout the organization.

Training and Development

To create a strengths-based culture, you'll want to alter the mission of the training and development function, too. We're accustomed to deficit-based development in our organizations, focused on improving weaknesses. In fact, there is a huge industry that provides training films, Webinars, CDs, workbooks, seminars, and courses designed to reduce weaknesses and deficiencies in our employees. Unfortunately, today, there are very few resources, tools, consultants, or materials designed to maximize strengths. (That's why we wrote this book!) It is important to consider, strategically, how we allocate training dollars in the organization. While weakness-based training may not disappear from organizations overnight—because we are so firmly grounded in our old paradigm of development—the key strategic question for training and development is, "How can we begin to replace deficit training with strength development?"

Succession Planning

Planning development for potential successors to key leadership roles—succession planning—is another lever to imbue the organization with strengths awareness. Many organizations are retooling their succession planning processes to focus on strengths. FedEx, for example, places strengths front and center in the succession planning process. Heather D'Alesandro, manager of leadership development and succession at FedEx Ground, told us in a 2007 interview:

> Focusing the executive team on strengths has shifted the discussion. It creates a vehicle where executives can more clearly see what an individual has to offer. It has opened a perspective that is deeper than a discussion about what *experience* they bring to the table and helped balanced their focus against key development areas. The discussion of strengths in succession

planning sessions also helps the executives to see how they can develop their high potentials across functions and disciplines. If particular strengths are critical to a job, then someone who demonstrates those strengths, but has no background in the function, may be the best candidate! We moved an individual who led an engineering group into the role of Director of the University, and replaced him in his engineering role with a woman who is not an engineer, because they had the best strengths profiles for the jobs!

Leadership: The Most Important People System Lever

When Andrea ran the Employee and Organization Development function at Novell, her clients would tell her, "We need to train our managers to lead." When she asked them what good leaders did and how they behaved, she drew blank stares. Finally, she went to the CEO with the question, "What does excellent leadership look like here at Novell?" Together, Andrea and the CEO began the process of creating a leadership competency model to answer it.

Leadership is practiced not so much in words as in attitude and in actions.
—Harold Geneen, founder,
MCI Communications

Noel Tichy, noted University of Michigan professor of business administration, described General Electric's (GE) Leadership Development Institute in Croton-on-Hudson, New York, as a "staging ground for corporate revolutions." He says it is a "key lever for radical transformation of GE's culture."[5] Leadership development is a fertile ground to plant the seeds of a strengths revolution!

233

If you want to radically change your organization to one that talks about strengths, identifies and applies strengths, and develops the strengths of individuals, teams, and the organization in its entirety, teach the organization's leaders to *lead*. Create a vision of what excellent leadership looks like in your organization, and work together with your leaders and managers to achieve the vision. Determine what strengths are needed to accomplish the vision and clarify the link between leaders' existing strengths and the desired leadership competence. In this way, leaders not only see what their leadership can accomplish, they also learn how to play to their strengths in the process. An excellent foundation to begin the leadership competency discussion is James M. Kouzes's and Barry Z. Posner's well-respected and often-applied leadership model found in their inspiring book, *The Leadership Challenge* (John Wiley & Sons, 2002). They identify the 5 Practices of Exemplary Leadership as:

1. *Model the Way*. Leaders must stand for something and believe in something. They must discover their own values and their own voice to express those values. They do what they say. They demonstrate the courage of their convictions and, not surprisingly, others are inspired to follow.

2. *Inspire a Shared Vision*. Leaders envision a desired future and then enlist others by appealing to and aligning with their visions and aspirations.

3. *Challenge the Process*. Leaders search for opportunities to change, grow, innovate, and improve. They take risks and create small wins that lead to bigger wins.

4. *Enable Others to Act*. Leaders build trust, foster collaboration, and promote cooperative goals. They strengthen others by sharing power and providing coaching, building others' competence and confidence.

5. *Encourage the Heart.* Leaders celebrate values and victories, recognize contributions (and strengths), express caring for their followers, and tap the hearts, passions, and aspirations of followers.

Teach your leaders to be *authentic.* Authentic leaders want to do what's right for their followers. Fred Luthans and Bruce Avolio, management scholars and research scientists, describe in detail the characteristics of authentic leaders. Their model is strong, vibrant, and presents a powerful vision for authentic leaders. Here's our summary of their six characteristics:

1. Authentic leaders believe each individual has something to offer. "One of the authentic leader's core challenges is to identify these strengths and help direct and build them appropriately."

2. Authentic leaders attempt to narrow the gap between their espoused values and their actions. To do this requires a deep understanding of their own values.

3. Authentic leaders openly discuss their vulnerabilities, thereby making room for associates to "complement the leader in terms of the strengths they bring to their collective challenges."

4. Authentic leaders go out in front, modeling "confidence, hope, optimism, and resiliency, which inspires others to action."

5. Authentic leaders view accomplishing the task and developing associates as equal in importance. When they begin to truly "walk the talk" of development, they grow themselves as well.

6. Authentic leaders approach situations with "shades of gray" by openly looking at all angles, sometimes changing their minds to be consistent with their authentic values.[6]

Teach your leaders to discover and apply their own strengths and the strengths of others. If you don't want merely 20 percent of your *people* using their strengths every day, you surely can't tolerate only 20 percent of your *leaders* using their strengths every day!

Culture

Changing the culture in any organization is "slow burn" work. Culture takes years to create. It takes even longer to change, because leaders have been hiring, rewarding, and developing people in the same ways—consistent with the defined culture—perhaps for decades. You can't change in a moment what took years to create.

Take, for example, the World Series of Poker (WSOP) Tournament. Amarillo Slim stood at the leader board of the 2000 WSOP Championship Round in Las Vegas and saw the name Kathy Liebert at the top. Amarillo Slim (real name: Preston Thomas) was a four-time WSOP winner, a lifelong professional gambler with a decidedly unsavory reputation, and a fixture at the tournament from its inception. A reporter reminded Amarillo that he once threatened to cut his own throat if a woman ever won the championship event.

The WSOP began in 1970 with a core of Texas professional gamblers—all men and all good old boys. Since 1970, the WSOP has had to adjust the culture of the tournament to embrace the ethnic and gender diversity of poker enthusiasts. For some folks, such as Amarillo Slim, this shift in the game was hard to accept. Gone are the days of the old gamblers club. Howard Greenbaum, vice president of Harrah's, said, in tribute to the diversity of the tournament, "Everybody wants to play in the World Series of Poker. It's dying and going to heaven for any poker player."[7]

Culture is defined by Kathy Ohm in her article "Leadership and Culture" as "the often hidden sets of norms and expectations that underlie what people 'expect' and see as 'expected of them' when they come to work. It is the set of often unspoken interactions, relationships, and expectations that spell out 'how we do business around here.'"

Business leaders may assume that their company's vision, values, and strategic priorities are synonymous with their company's culture. Unfortunately, too often the vision, strategy, and shared values may only be words hanging on a plaque on the wall. They too soon suffer "death by lamination"!

While employees can see and experience elements of culture that include artifacts (such as corporate logowear and Successories plaques on many desktops) or rituals (such as casual Fridays and bagels for team meetings), the far more powerful aspects of corporate culture are invisible. The cultural core is comprised of the beliefs, values, standards, paradigms, worldviews, moods, and private conversations of the people. Culture is the foundation for all actions and decisions within a team, department, or organization.

Culture is complex and can be "mushy." The keys to changing a culture to actively build strengths are:

- ♠ Play to your organization's strengths.
- ♠ Champion your vision, strategy, and shared values.
- ♠ Design meaningful work.
- ♠ Share power—and empower.

PLAY TO YOUR ORGANIZATION'S STRENGTHS

Because you're this far in our book, you know what this means. Playing to your strengths begins with discovering and applying your own strengths, then doing the same with your followers. It includes aligning and building the strengths in your teams, and clarifying and articulating the organization's strengths. Shine your light on the strengths of the organization. Look deeper than the best skills of the organization or your market niche. Look at who you are as an organization—those inherent strengths that make your organization so capable.

Is your organization's strength its employees' love for fun? Picture Disney and Columbia Sportswear! Is it unbounded innovation? Imagine Toyota's design center or Google's new business channels team. Is it analysis? Think RAND Corporation or the Brookings Institute. What strengths create *your* organization's unique differentiator?

Beyond *identifying* your organization's natural strengths, it's important to *nurture* them to truly support a strengths-based culture. In every conversation, in every meeting, and in every process, leaders in the organization must capitalize on strengths. To illustrate, every year, a nonprofit organization in Carol's community sells raffle tickets to win a Porsche. This is an important fundraiser for the organization. Last year, they sold fewer raffle tickets than the year before, and the committee planned a meeting to discuss "what went wrong." While the session started as a depressing conversation about all sorts of things outside the fundraising committee's control, fortunately it turned around when the leader asked, "Okay, what went *right*?" Soon they discovered patterns of when the most tickets sold, in what settings, and with what audiences. The committee developed actions for next year targeted toward increasing these successful circumstances. Shortly thereafter, the committee's energy returned and they were committed to a plan of action.

Internal-change agents can further the organization-wide strengths agenda with effective processes like these and an attentive, powerful mind set. Whether they are organization development consultants, quality professionals, HR reps, or meeting facilitators in your organization, urge them to begin—and continue—asking, "What went right? Now, how do we create more of that?"

CHAMPION YOUR VISION, STRATEGY, AND SHARED VALUES

As we write this, we are working with leaders in a major corporation that is changing its culture. A new CEO has been a driving force in this work, although the team itself, before the new CEO arrived, saw how the culture was slowing down the organization. Efforts bubbled to the surface throughout the last year to make the culture more innovative, nimble, and high performing, while building on the strengths of the organization's brands, history, and employees.

Of all the processes this organization is using to drive changes in the culture—training, management meetings, gathering input and ideas, posting new concepts on its intranet, and adapting structures and systems—nothing has been as powerful as the new CEO championing his own view of the desired culture. This particular CEO talks in terms of the characteristics that every employee should possess and demonstrate. Unique characteristics such as humility, compassion, and curiosity are among the traits he touts as vital to the organization going forward. As soon as the CEO began using these words, the corporate lore took over. Stories began to shape themselves and spread like wildfire. "He's talking about humility! What does that mean? How do we do it?" These stories intrigue employees, and encourage them to see and experience not only a new way of "being" at work, but also the incredible new possibilities that come with it.

Likewise, another client firm is changing its culture, though less consciously. The new CEO is creating a shift in focus from a very "customer-focused, do-the-right-thing" kind of culture to a culture driven by measurement and the bottom line. Unfortunately, this shift in corporate culture has closed people down. It's scary for folks—it seems less about them and their passion for their work, and more about some impersonal measurements.

Senior leadership's power to change the culture, by just a few words and actions, is a force to be reckoned with! It is still a slow burn; deep change takes time. The organization can and will help accelerate adoption of the strengths-based culture change if senior leadership states a compelling vision that aligns with the values of organization members.

Good leaders begin to shift the culture by speaking to a vision that engages and persuades others. Powerful visions are shaped by senior executives and developed through widespread conversation with the workforce. We urge you to capture your organization's culture as clearly as you can through a powerful story—your vision of the desired future. Base it upon shared values to achieve maximum commitment to it—especially if the new vision requires a change that feels jarring.

The life I touch for good or ill will touch another life, and that in turn another, until who knows where the trembling stops or in what far place my touch will be felt.
—Frederick Buechner

A visionary leader can be transformational. Visions make membership in an organization special, enriching, and meaningful. According to Aristotle, there are three compelling elements to persuasion, and thus, to an engaging vision: logos, ethos, and pathos.

- ♠ **Logos** is logic, reason, intellectual analysis, and the ability to provide solid rationale for an action. Leaders engage others by outlining the logic and reasoning behind their initiative.

- ♠ **Ethos** is ethics, character, morality; a sense of justice. Leaders engage others by identifying the importance of the issue and emphasizing its moral meaning.

- ♠ **Pathos** is emotional appeal, empathy; touching or sentimentally moving. Leaders engage others by sharing what the vision means to them personally, not hesitating to speak their own passion for the vision.

DESIGN MEANINGFUL WORK

There is a direct link between meaningful work and focusing on strengths. When we apply our strengths, we have the potential to create work—and a way of working—that enhances personal success, fulfillment, and meaning, whether we perceive our work as a job, a career, or a calling. When we have the opportunity to apply our strengths every day, we are more engaged.

There are two ways to increase meaning at work. The first is to promote the shared values, vision, and strategic goals of the organization. Having a clear understanding of what is valued by the organization helps employees align their work with the organization's goals. If they hear consistently that "do the right thing," "delightful customer experience," "curiosity," or "make the best use of our strengths" is a value commonly shared across the organization, they will find harmony between their internally held values and the values of the organization—or they will experience dissonance and leave. Either way, you are creating greater alignment between the employees who stay and the goals of the organization. Reinforce the shared values, vision, and strategic goals frequently—in written documents, in presentations, and speeches, and on the organization's intranet. Most importantly, ensure that all leaders and managers know how to help individuals align their own performance goals with the organization's goals, creating meaning and purpose in the work they do.

The second lever to create meaningful work may surprise you a bit. To foster meaningfulness at work, build intentional communities. As individuals, we have a need to belong to and be part of a community. You can encourage communities of practice, cross-functional teams, or high-performing workgroups to form and develop as communities. Why these affinity groups gather is based on any number of reasons—common goals, interests, backgrounds, projects, areas of specialization, and so on. We know of communities in organizations gathering around a plethora of topics, from dog rescue to quality improvement, from women in leadership to internal change agents to one community that calls itself "geeks." Shared common interests will naturally

241

lead people to share their strengths, while making the content of the work itself more meaningful.

SHARE POWER—AND EMPOWER

Give employees the power to shape their roles and apply their strengths. Power sharing, power shifting, and empowering employees to make decisions about how they design their role and perform their work builds a greater reliance on strengths, and increases opportunities for strengths to show up.

All of these components of culture link together, of course. Creating a strong vision, strategy, and shared values—as well as increasing the meaningfulness of work and sharing power—builds the organization's capacity and its vitality, its ability and eagerness to act.

Leaders in any organization have power, in part, because they have formal authority. But power isn't a finite resource. When leaders share power with their employees, by giving them the appropriate authority and autonomy to make decisions about their work, they redefine the relationships and increase the total amount of power in the organization. Sharing power like this increases the total vitality across the organization as well. This, of course, is good for employees, leaders, and the capacity of the organization overall. Managers and leaders at all levels can shift their power orientation from one of "power over" to one of "power with," and increase the organization's total power.

Organization design is also a lever for changing power dynamics. Organizations with strong hierarchies can hold all the power near the top of the organization, requiring decisions about resources or goals or tactics to rise up in the organization for approval, and then filter back down for execution. Historically, we think of organization design as the structure for information flow and decision-making. What if we designed organizations not only in light of how information and decisions travel, but also to build strong communities, high-quality relationships, and excellence in communication (not just information sharing)? The structure of the organization can foster or inhibit connections among employees. With good connection, people respond positively to one another and share ideas—essential when their work is interdependent.

Another client of ours, a transportation firm, is redesigning its organization. The business units are shifting from a geographic to a service-based focus. Now, instead of one business unit serving a major geography, there will be three business units offering three unique services to a wider geography. This shift makes a lot of sense to the organization and to the employees, because it aligns employee skills and strengths while establishing relationships among those employees who offer similar services.

Managers can redesign at all levels of the organization, if the leadership shares the power! For example, human resource functions in recent years have aligned to the internal customers they serve, rather than being isolated as an administrative service, as in the traditional model of HR. The role of the HR business partner is to understand the internal client so well that she can broker services such as recruiting, compensation, or training as needed. An interesting outcome of this popular structure, in addition to internal clients receiving better service, is that the HR professionals are able to say, "I don't have that skill—but I can bring in someone who does," thereby increasing reliance on their own strengths, and counting on the strengths of colleagues to fill in the gaps.

EMPOWER A CHANGE LEADERSHIP TEAM

Charter a team to champion and lead the change to a strengths-based culture. Consider the strengths you need to lead change effectively, and the strengths in the hands of the players in your organization. Ignore job titles; look at strengths. Perhaps Joe from HR holds the J♠, and Christine, your CFO, has the ace. Maybe Rafael, a manager from sales, holds the 10♠, while Beth and George from engineering bring the K♠ and Q♠. You've combined five disparate individuals with the requisite strengths, formed a cross-functional team, and created a royal flush!

Go All In

A major package transportation firm, a sizeable healthcare organization, a revered high technology company, a transit company lauded for its innovation...these are examples of the many companies among our clients whose leaders are applying the concepts of strengths in their organizations. They have chosen to make significant shifts in their processes to engage strengths—a new imperative that crosses industries, technologies, companies, and nonprofit organizations as well.

The challenge for all of us is that strength-based development is cutting-edge work! We haven't always been able to reveal the organization names of our clients because, for them, this work is proprietary—a differentiator and a strategic advantage in the marketplace. And yet, the Strengths Revolution is happening everywhere! With more than 2 million people completing the Clifton StrengthsFinder, and 850,000 more completing the VIA Signature Strengths tool, we know the concepts have spread far and wide among individuals. Our job is to capitalize on this groundswell.

We look forward to academics, practitioners, and organizations publishing their learning and their results when they strategically apply strengths in their organizations. We would like to house a repository for such exciting stories of change! Now that you know your own strengths, and how to commit your "full house" to receive spectacular results for yourself and others, please visit our Website and add your wisdom and your story to the dialogue!

Implementation Ideas

Assess the Strengths of Your Organization

Doing a SWOT analysis is one way to gather the strengths of the organization. In a SWOT, the team explores the Strengths, Weaknesses, Opportunities, and Threats that currently exist in the organization, and in the context in which it operates. A SWOT analysis tool is available on our Website.

Tweak or Radically Change Your Systems and Culture

If you are a senior leader in an organization, or an HR professional at most any level, first, learn and apply your own strengths! Then, review your organization's systems and culture and consider tweaking these components to create a strengths-based organization:

- ♠ Systems that attract, acquire, and onboard employees.
- ♠ Systems that asses performance and reward.
- ♠ Systems that develop capability.
- ♠ The leadership competency model.
- ♠ Culture: Play to your organization's strengths.
- ♠ Culture: Recreate your vision, strategy, and shared values.
- ♠ Culture: Support meaningful work.
- ♠ Culture: Share power and empower others.

Change Your Local Culture

If you are a leader at a lower level in an organization, change your own systems and your local culture. Don't wait for your organization to make a major paradigm shift. Create a strengths-based culture in your own team or department.

WATCH *Dirty Jobs*

Watch *Dirty Jobs* on the Discovery Channel, or read Studs Terkel's wonderful book of interviews with workers in all types of occupations titled, *Working* (New Press, 1997).

CHALLENGE YOUR OWN LEADERSHIP

Read *The Leadership Challenge* by James M. Kouzes and Barry Z. Posner. While you're at it, check out *The Leadership Workbook, The Leadership Planner, The Leadership Practices Inventory*, and the *Encouraging the Heart Workbook*, all by Kouzes and Posner, available at their Website, *www.leadershipchallenge.com* or at *www.amazon.com*.

Enjoy an interesting article

A recent article in *Harvard Business Review* considers how "complementary leadership"—leadership that combines more than one executive's strengths, sometimes coleading from the same role and title—is built on four essential pillars: a common vision and strategy, common performance incentives, communication and coordination, and mutual trust. Take a look at "The Leadership Team: Complementary Strengths or Conflicting Agendas," in *Harvard Business Review*, Harvard Business Press, April 2007, pages 90–98.

CHAPTER NINE

ROYAL FLUSH:

PLAYING YOUR BEST HAND IN THE MOST IMPORTANT GAME

Royal Flush: An Ace-high straight of the same suit;
a Royal Flush is the best possible hand in poker.

Warren Buffet confounded a number of his observers when he donated a sizable portion of his personal wealth ($31 billion) to the Bill and Melinda Gates Foundation. People wondered why he wouldn't want to manage his donations himself. When asked, Buffet replied, "They can give it away better than I can. Besides, philanthropy isn't fun for me. Running my business day-to-day is fun for me. Philanthropy just isn't something I enjoy thinking about every day."[1] It takes a great deal of self-understanding, strength of character, and self-possession to confess that philanthropy bores you. Buffet, known for his wisdom and talent, admitted, "Philanthropy weakens me, and it always will, so I am choosing to hand it off to someone who is strengthened by it. I admire the goals of philanthropy. In fact I admire them so much that I cannot allow them to be undertaken by a guy like me."[2]

Warren Buffet understands strengths, and chooses to play his Royal Flush—his best hand possible—in the arena that makes the greatest use of his strengths. But he doesn't stop there. He also chooses to apply his resources—the money he has earned through direct application of his strengths—to have a bigger impact in the world.

What about you? Have you ever asked yourself, "Am I making a real difference in the world? Am I touching as many lives as I can? Do I have an ache or longing to share my strengths further in the world?"

Twenty years from now you will be more disappointed by the things you didn't do than by the ones you did do. So throw off the bowlines. Sail away from the safe harbour, catch the trade winds in your sales.
Explore. Dream. Discover.
—Mark Twain

Throughout this book, we have challenged you to make a difference by applying your strengths at work. Now we're challenging you to apply them in the most important game of all—the game of *life*.

What Is Your Calling?

In Chapter 8♠, we talked about the difference between a job, a career, and a calling. You may recall that people who view work as a "job" focus on the material rewards of work, not on meaning or fulfillment. People with a career orientation work for the increased pay, prestige, and status that comes through promotion and advancement. Those who view their work as a "calling" work for fulfillment and see the work as an end to itself, believing their work makes the world a better place.

If your work is your calling, congratulations! You experience the emotional rewards of well-chosen work and the financial rewards as well! If your work is not your calling, what is? Do you find your calling when working with children? In protecting the environment? Among survivors of domestic violence in your community? What passions have you put aside while pursuing gainful employment?

Now that you can genuinely use your strengths to further your career satisfaction, what contribution can you make to others? As a citizen of the world, with new knowledge of your strengths and weaknesses, you have a profound opportunity—and, many believe, a responsibility—to engage your strengths and positively affect people and the planet. In all walks of life and circumstances, individuals, organizations, and communities can benefit from the self-esteem and self-empowerment that occurs when we know and use our strengths. The slice of the world you have passion for awaits your leadership. We urge you, as a leader, to become an advocate for strengths.

We are eager to see how you choose to apply your innate talents and gifts, and we're excited for you to teach others to discover their strengths! We challenge you to think broader and deeper about the affect you can have in the world. Of course, it's your choice to accept or decline our challenge.

Anyone can participate in a walk/run event to raise money for cancer research; anyone can donate a personal item to a charity auction; anyone can volunteer to assist on a project with a good cause. As important as these contributions may be, if your contribution is *not* utilizing your unique gifts, you won't have the same affect as if you contributed your strength to a project or program needing that exact strength.

*Your work is to discover your work
and then with all your heart to give
yourself to it.*
—Buddha

A number of years ago, Carol leveraged her strengths—those of visioning and engaging others—to create with four friends a networking group for women leaders in St. George, Utah. The group meets quarterly for happy hour and dinner to support each other's businesses, to mentor each other, to connect with intelligent minds, to boost each other's spirits, to forge friendships, and so on. At its inception, the founding team committed to keep the operation of the group easy and joyful. They took the time to thoughtfully discuss the tasks required to administer the group and meetings, and they identified the key role each founder would play in order to leverage her unique strengths.

After five years, the group has grown to more than 200 members, and the founders agree that meetings continue to be both simple and delightful to manage. Each founder contributes from her strengths of vision, influence, connection, compassion, design, and/or humor to welcome new members, facilitate meetings, and maintain an easy and effective Web presence. The founders feel honored and delighted to contribute their strengths to connect with and help other women. Their successful networking group brings value to the women of St. George, and it remains a smooth-running, virtually self-sustaining operation today.

So, don't go out and spend time on a charity event or in a volunteer role just for charity's sake.

Give the charity your *strengths*, and have a meaningful and potent impact by bringing your best to the most important game of all—your life.

> ♠
>
> *If I am not for myself, who will be for me? If I am only for myself, who am I? If not now, when?*
> *—Hillel*
>
> ♠

Mentoring

We propose three broad ways for you to apply your strengths, and your knowledge about uncovering and developing them: mentoring, serving your community, and creating and leaving a legacy for those who follow. We realize, too, that these three opportunities may, and probably will, overlap. When you choose how to play your best hand—your royal flush—you may discover yourself applying your strengths across a broad range of situations and opportunities that had not previously occurred to you.

Mentoring is a natural application for your strengths knowledge. All around us there are worthy individuals who would blossom with a mentor to help them claim their strengths. Of course, you can seek and find many mentoring opportunities at work. You can look for younger or less-experienced individuals ready to benefit from a sagacious leader like you to help them learn the ropes, understand their strengths, and be enormously successful in their own calling.

Our client Gregory reached out to a woman in another department. Gregory interacted with Holly occasionally in project team meetings. Holly brought a unique skill set to the projects that Gregory led. Gregory could see that Holly was a diamond in the rough, who, with a little mentoring, would shine! He invited her to lunch and asked if she would be interested in a mentoring relationship with him. She enthusiastically agreed.

Gregory began by ensuring that Holly understood the larger context of her work and how it contributed to the organization's mission. In their next session, Gregory asked Holly to assess her performance in her role—notably, where she felt she made the greatest contribution and where she felt less confident or competent. They discussed how she might gather more information from internal clients, her team, and her boss to add more perspective to her answers.

Gregory then coached Holly into a clearer understanding of her strengths, using the steps from Chapter 6♠. Gregory and Holly worked for a number of weeks on aligning her strengths to her role, expanding her role to make greater use of her strengths, and managing her weaknesses. Gregory did this because one of *his* strengths is developing people, and he experienced great satisfaction by supporting Holly. He also received the benefits of her expanding confidence and competence when she performed even better as a member of their project team.

A mentor offers advice and guidance to the mentee. In organizations, a mentor guides, supports, and enables by helping mentees assess themselves while they learn how to maneuver in the organization. A mentor may also provide access to key people in the organization or the industry because of his place inside the system.

A mentor-mentee relationship can also exist outside of the work environment. Another client, Paul, after gaining a thorough understanding of his strengths and crafting his job to maximize them, began to see that he had a perspective and knowledge to offer young adults as well. He recently became a Big Brother to a young man living in a residential unit for troubled teens. It is difficult to assess who gains more satisfaction from the relationship.

> ♠
>
> *By learning you will teach;*
> *by teaching you will learn.*
> —*Latin Proverb*
>
> ♠

Chip Huge, a colleague of ours who is a certified coach, works with teens who have acted out through drugs or violence, and with young adults who want a greater sense of self-direction. Chip helps them see how great they are. In his coaching with these kids, he uses the Highlands Ability Battery (*www.highlandsco.com*), a tool that helps young people see—sometimes for the first time in their lives—their real strengths and talents. He helps them gain the self-awareness and confidence they need to act in ways consistent with what they *really* want to have happen in their lives. Chip assists them in becoming high-functioning and contributing members of society.

Just as important—and extremely important for these kids—Chip also works with their parents. He helps parents see the gifts, talents, and strengths of their kids, and he teaches them to support their children in becoming who they are capable of being. This requires parents to rely on their own strengths to communicate with and support their children. Thus, the strengths of both the young adult and the parents are the keys to this new way of seeing our children's untapped potential!

Chip has carved himself a niche that makes full use of his own strengths, and he makes a very tangible difference in the world. We wanted you to meet Chip now, because he inspires us to wonder how can we, as strong leaders, do what he is doing in our communities. Who can we help grow and develop, by applying our strengths to their circumstances? Who do you know—an individual, a group, or an organization—that needs your care, your attention, your servant leadership, and your strengths?

Serving Your Community

It hardly needs repeating—utilizing our strengths in our communities is a powerful way to have a big impact in the world. And because using our strengths is fun as well as fruitful, community service need not feel like an obligation or a burden. Instead, we can build our competence in our strength while serving others.

There are, of course, many ways to define community, and an infinite number of ways to apply your strengths! It's your choice. "Community" may be your neighborhood, or the city or town in which you live. You may see your community as a country, or even the world. Your community may be professional, or based on one of your passions. It doesn't matter how you define your community of interest; it just matters that you do.

We have clients who see their community as the neighborhood in which their kids are growing up, such as IT professionals in this country; global bus and light rail providers; members of their church; the homeless in the city in which they work; or other members of AA. The definition of "community" is as varied as clients themselves. Which of your communities is ready for your strengths?

The stories we could tell are endless. Our friend Carolyn is motivated and inspired by her biggest strength of connection—having both a deep desire to connect with others as well as a commitment to connecting others. She not only started her own nonprofit organization, but every day she connects people in her community with others who might serve the accomplishment of their visions. One of our clients holds a corporate job and is an excellent musician. He created a program to build self-esteem through music, and offers it to advantaged and disadvantaged kids in his community. Another

You are not here merely to make a living. You are here to enable the world to live more amply, with greater vision, and with a finer spirit of home and achievement. You are here to enrich the world. You impoverish yourself if you forget this errand.
—Woodrow Wilson

client is an orthopedist who just graced the front page of her local paper for her volunteer work with patients in Nepal. We have a client with strong organizing skills and a passion for animals; she started a rescue program for Brittany and Springer Spaniel dogs. Our friend Mark runs his own IT consulting business and also chose to run for city council. Mark's marketing and organizing strengths are proving useful to a community dealing with significant growth issues. Our colleague, Mary, chose to apply her strengths of seeing the big picture and identifying strengths in others to join a volunteer board working with domestic violence survivors in her community.

Take a look at your checkbook. What non-profit or community service receives money from you, consistently and regularly? Think about where you've volunteered before, and ask what satisfaction you did—or did not—receive from it. Go back to the exercise you completed in Chapter 4♠ when you brainstormed a huge list of possible careers, roles, or jobs associated with your unique combination of strengths. What does your list reveal to you? How can you apply your strengths to your passion?

Your contribution can be big or small, life-changing, or simply life improving. It doesn't matter. We don't want you to contribute from a place of "I should"—but rather, from that deep place where your passion intersects your strengths.

We aren't asking you to quit your job, stop providing for your family, or live off the grid. We are just asking you to look through two lenses—first is the lens of your strengths and second is the lens of your compassionate heart—and choose to serve your community from your powerful, generous, and strong self. The gift of our strengths is a gift of ourselves and is profound indeed.

Leaving a Legacy

We believe the seeds of our legacy are planted and nurtured by our strengths. You are leaving something behind for those who follow in your footsteps. What are you leaving? What will people say about you when you are gone? In what way will you leave the world a better place for having lived here?

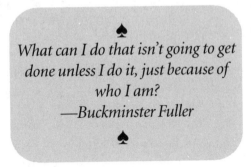

What can I do that isn't going to get done unless I do it, just because of who I am?
—Buckminster Fuller

The American Heritage Dictionary defines legacy as, "Something handed down from an ancestor or a predecessor or from the past."[3] There is a legacy inside each of us, eager to soar.

We each have a gift to give. Certainly, excellence in leading people is a gift. Raising happy children is also an extremely important gift. *But what if there is more?* What if there is something lying dormant within you just waiting to ignite?

It's exciting to realize that we all leave a legacy—whether we are conscious of it or not. We leave something to a generation that follows, whether it is a physical generation—your children and your children's children—or a community or professional generation.

A legacy doesn't need to be so big or impressive that they dedicate a monument to you at the state capitol. Though it could be! It doesn't need to be a great work of literature. Though it might be! Your legacy may be a new program or a better process in your organization. It may be unrelated to work—perhaps building a better skateboard park in your town, or making a difference in the life of a disadvantaged child.

When we ask people about their legacies, the reaction is typically a sharp intake of breath with an increase in anxiety. "How can you ask such a big question? I have no idea what my legacy will be!" However, we suspect a legacy is not something we decide on when we're 92 years old. While you may be able to tweak it at that time, your legacy is something you leave behind every day. How is your world better because you are here? Are there people who have found new insights, resources, and strength because they know you? Have you shared your gifts and talents? Have you used them for your own good and the good of those you love—as well as to change a corner of the world? If you die tomorrow, what is the contribution by which you will be remembered? Did you inspire others? Perhaps you have cleaned up the planet in your own small way. Perhaps you encouraged young girls to enter science, or introduced city dwellers to the wonders of the wilderness. Or, perhaps you helped to establish a food pantry in your town, took in a scared, abandoned, pregnant teenager, or washed cars to raise money for the Humane Society.

What is the legacy you choose to leave, and are you choosing it consciously—or by default? Take a few moments and consider what impact you have already made through the unique strengths you have shared. Don't be shy! This reflection just may embolden your legacy!

Life Purpose

This conversation about mentoring, community service, and legacy inextricably links with life purpose.

A life purpose is foundational and, along with your values, passions, and strengths, serves to guide you as you make the rest of your life the best of your life.

Marty Seligman, the Positive Psychology expert, talks about three kinds of lives and their relationship to life satisfaction. The "pleasurable life" is about accumulating as many "kicks" as you can, and

Your time is limited, so don't waste it living someone else's life...don't let the noise of others' opinions drown out your own inner voice. And most important, have the courage to follow your heart and intuition. They somehow already know what you truly want to become. Everything else is secondary.
—Steve Jobs

learning to savor and appreciate them. Pleasure comes from shopping, food, meaningless sex, and so forth. You may not be surprised to learn that research shows more pleasure does not correlate with more life satisfaction.

The "good life" is about understanding and using one's core strengths and virtues in work and at play. The good life *does* correlate with measures of life satisfaction.

Finally, the "meaningful life" occurs when a person uses his strengths for the purpose of something larger than himself. Choosing to live a life of purpose or meaning has the highest correlation with life satisfaction.[4]

We're proposing that you have an opportunity to increase your life satisfaction by declaring your life purpose. Not a bad challenge or opportunity! We ask all of our clients about their purpose, and most do not have an answer. Somewhere along the way, we learned that purpose is something given to us—a calling from God, a voice in the wilderness, a path that suddenly presents itself. Life purpose is not something you *find,* magically, by invoking a spell with your wand (ala Harry Potter!). Your life purpose is something you *choose.* You craft, design, and create your purpose from your experiences, intuition, interests, passions, values, and strengths. You create such inner clarity and focus that your purpose reveals itself. By the way, many of our clients who *do* answer the question will talk about their children—being the best father they can be, or raising children to be happy, contributing members of society, with strong values. We ask, "How well are you living today to demonstrate what a happy and contributing member of society looks like? Are you a role model of an adult totally aligned with his or her values, and intentionally choosing to live on purpose? Do your children see a purposeful life that contributes in whatever way its heart is called to contribute?"

A life purpose doesn't have to be cast in concrete. After all, your life is a work in progress! Your life purpose, however, does have to be an over-arching goal that guides you to contribute your gifts in the most compelling way. For 20 years, Andrea saw her life purpose as "making organizations really great places to live." Throughout time, her passions shifted a bit to her current life purpose, "ceating and holding space for leaders to grow." It doesn't matter that the purpose of her life changed. What matters is that she attempts to contribute and make a difference.

You don't get to choose how you're going to die, or when. You can only decide how you're going to live now.
—*Joan Baez*

Choose your life purpose. Don't wait for a calling. That phone battery is dead. You have to recharge it with intention, action, and choice.

The following are a few more questions you might want to explore as you consider how best to apply your strengths:

♠ What three things happening in the world today inspire and excite you?

♠ What three things are you most angry about in the world today?

♠ If you had all the time, money, and resources you need at your disposal, what one problem would you most like to address—most like to solve—in the world? It may be something in your community, in your country, or in the world. Bigger is not necessarily better. Think globally, act locally.

♠ What impact would you create by solving that problem?

♠ What would creating that impact on the world give to you?

♠ What do your responses to these questions tell you about your purpose in life?

A classic question to engage your sense of life purpose is to imagine one phrase you choose to have written on your tombstone. What will it be? Really, stop and create that phrase right now. For what notion or cause did you take a stand?

What do you hope others will say about you at your wake? Especially consider what people will say who are not in your immediate family. What do you want your colleagues to say? Your clients? Members of your community? Your friends? Your enemies?

Our clients who can answer the question, "What is your life purpose?" often say, "To make a difference." We emphatically suggest that that is not enough to guide conscious action. The question is, "What is the explicit difference you choose to make in the world?" The compelling answer is very specific, and weaves itself within the fabric of your strengths. (There's more guidance on how to create your purpose statement on our Website.)

Play to Your Strengths: Your Royal Flush

We invite, encourage, cajole, and urge you to discover your strengths and apply them in your world. We know beyond a shadow of a doubt that playing to your strengths will bring you deep joy, satisfaction, fulfillment, achievement, growth, and profound success. As a leader, playing to your strengths is even more important, because you affect so many others. So, teach them to play to their strengths, and together we'll create a better, stronger world.

A

Implementation Ideas

PLAY YOUR BEST HAND IN THE MOST IMPORTANT GAME

Throughout this chapter, we have offered many questions for your consideration as you choose where and how to apply your strengths. Some questions will inspire you; others will likely have little resonance. We repeat the most salient of these questions below. Choose two, three, six, or eight that speak to you. Mull them over for a while. Take them out for a walk in the wilderness. Write about them in a journal or type up your responses. Then, let them move and inspire you to action!

- ♠ Are you making a real difference in the world?
- ♠ Are you touching as many lives as you can?
- ♠ Do you have an ache or a longing to share your strengths further in the world?
- ♠ If your work is not your calling, what is?
- ♠ What passions have you put aside while pursuing gainful employment?
- ♠ Now that you can genuinely use your strengths to further your career satisfaction, what contribution can you make to others?
- ♠ Who do you know—an individual, a group, an organization—in need of your care, your attention, your servant leadership, and your strengths?

♠ Which of your communities is ready for your strengths?

♠ What non-profit or community service receives money from you, consistently and regularly?

Go back to the exercise you completed in Chapter 4♠ when you brainstormed a huge list of possible careers, roles, or jobs associated with your unique combination of strengths.

♠ What does your list reveal to you?

♠ How can you apply your strengths to your passion?

♠ What will people say about you when you are gone? In what way will you leave the world a better place for having lived here?

♠ Have you shared your gifts and talents?

♠ Have you used them for your own good and the good of those you love—as well as to change a corner of the world?

♠ If you die tomorrow, what is the legacy by which you will be remembered?

♠ What is the legacy you choose to leave, and are you choosing it consciously—or by default?

♠ How well are you living today to demonstrate to your children what a happy and contributing member of society looks like? Are you a role model of an adult totally aligned with his or her values, and intentionally choosing to live on purpose?

♠ Do your children see a purposeful life that contributes in whatever way its heart is called to contribute?

♠ What three things happening in the world today inspire and excite you?

♠ What three things are you most angry about in the world today?

- ♠ If you had all the time, money, and resources you need at your disposal, what one problem would you most like to address—most like to solve—in the world?

- ♠ What affect or impact would you create by solving that problem?

- ♠ What would creating that impact on the world give to you?

- ♠ What do your responses to these questions tell you about your purpose in life?

- ♠ For what notion or cause did you take a stand?

- ♠ What do you hope others will say about you at your wake? What do you want your colleagues to say? Your clients? Members of your community? Your friends? Your enemies?

- ♠ What is the *explicit* difference you choose to make in the world?

PICK A NEW BOOK OFF THE SHELF

Vital Friends: The People You Can't Afford to Live Without by Tom Rath (Gallup Press, 2006).

Savoring: A New Model of Positive Experience, by Bryant & Verfoff (Lawrence Erlbaum Associates, 2006), about savoring life versus coping.

The Power of Purpose: Creating Meaning in Your Life and Work, by Richard J. Leider (Berrett-Koehler Publishers, 2005).

A Leader's Legacy, by James M. Kouzes and Barry Z. Posner (Jossey-Bass, 2006).

Learned Optimism: How to Change Your Mind and Your Life, by Martin E.P. Seligman, Ph.D. (The Free Press, 1990, 1998).

Notes

Chapter 1♠

1. We are grateful to www.pokernews.com and www.pokersyte.com for all of the poker definitions in *Play to Your Strengths*.
2. Purnell, *The Today Show*. (As spoken by Marcus Buckingham)
3. Ibid.
4. Harter and Schmidt. "Business Unit Level Relationship Between Employee Satisfaction, Employee Engagement, and Business Outcomes." *Journal of Applied Psychology*: 268–279.
5. Buckingham. *Go Put Your Strengths to Work*.
6. Peterson and Park. *Psychological Inquiry*:141–146.
7. DeRoo and DeRoo. *What's Right With Me*.
8. Peterson Park, Nansook. *Journal of Organizational Behavior*: 1149–1154.
9. Purnell, *The Today Show*.

Chapter 2♠

1. A Better Way to Work™

2. Shepard, *Working With Careers*: 179–180.

3. Quinn, Robert. *Harvard Business Review*: 77–83.

Chapter 4♠

1. Gilbert. http://news.com.com/2100-1022_3-5740885.html.

2. *An Inconvenient Truth*. http://climatecrisis.org.

3. Hawkins. *Power vs. Force*.

4. "Understanding James Woods www.toppoker.org/poker-players/james-woods.html.

5. Buckingham. *Go Put Your Strengths to Work*.

6. Buckingham and Clifton. *Now, Discover Your Strengths*.

Chapter 5♠

1. Garcia. Poker Player Online. www.pokerplayernewspaper.com/.

2. Buckingham. *Go Put Your Strengths to Work*.

3. Blanchflower. Dartmouth College Department of Economics.

4. Gore. *Navigating Change*.

Chapter 6♠

1. We are grateful to the leaders at the Coaches Training Institute for this powerful perspective that shifts all of our coaching conversations. (www.thecoaches.com)

2. Gladwell. *Blink*.

3. Whitmore. *Coaching for Performance*.

Chapter 7♠

1. Shaw. *Group Dynamics*.

2. Katzenbach and Smith. *The Wisdom of Teams*.

3. Buckingham. *Go Put Your Strengths to Work*.

Chapter 8♠

1. Black. "The Road to Recovery." *Gallup Management Journal*:10-12.

2. Cameron, Dutton, and Quinn. *Positive Organizational Scholarship*: Ch. 8.

3. Ibid.

4. Ibid.

5. Tichy. "GE's Crotonville: A Staging Ground for Corporate Revolutions." *Academy of Management Executive*: 99–106.

6. Luthans and Avolio. *Authentic Leadership*: Chapter 16.

7. Grotenstein and Reback. *All In*.

8. Ohm. "Leadership and Culture: the close connection." www.thefreelibrary.com/_/print/PrintArticle.aspx?id=152994006.

Chapter 9♠

1. Buckingham. *Go Put Your Strengths to Work*.

2. Ibid.

3. Pickett. *The American Heritage Dictionary*.

4. Pladott. "Positive Psychology and Positive Organizational Scholarship." www.ontrackcoaching.com/articles/positivepsychology.htm.

BIBLIOGRAPHY

An Inconvenient Truth. http://climatecrisis.org. (Accessed April 19, 2007.)

Better Way to Work, A™—Achieving Fulfillment, Sustainability & Success Using the 7 Entrepreneurial Skills™. A workshop manual published by Entrevis® 2005, *www.Entrevis.com.*

Black, Brad. "The Road to Recovery." *Gallup Management Journal* 1 (2001):10–12.

Blanchflower, David, and Andrew Oswald. "Measuring Latent Entrepreneurship Across Nations." Research summary paper. Dartmouth College Department of Economics, January, 2000.

Brim, Brian. "Probing the Dark Side of Employees' Strengths." *Gallup Management Journal.* February 8, 2007. *http://gmj.gallup.com/content/default.aspx?ci=26365.* (Accessed May 4, 2007.)

Buckingham, Marcus and Donald O. Clifton. *Now, Discover Your Strengths.* New York: The Free Press, 2001.

Buckingham, Marcus. *Go Put Your Strengths to Work: Six Powerful Ways to Achieve Outstanding Performance.* New York: The Free Press, 2007.

Cameron, K.S., J.E. Dutton, and R.E. Quinn, eds. *Positive Organizational Scholarship.* San Francisco, Calif.: Berrett-Koehler Publishers, Inc., 2003.

Clifton, Donald and Paula Nelson. *Soar with your Strengths.* New York: Dell, 1995.

Clifton, Donald O. and James K. Harter. Chapter 8: Investing in Strengths from Positive Organizational Scholarship. San Francisco, Calif.: Berrett-Koehler Publishers, Inc., 2003.

Collins, Jim. *Good to Great.* New York: Harper Collins, 2001.

Connors, Roger, Tom Smith, and Craig Hickman. *The Oz Principle: Getting Results Through Individual and Organizational Accountability.* Paramus, N.J.: Prentice Hall Press, 2004.

Covey, Stephen R. *The 7 Habits of Highly Effective People.* New York: Simon & Schuster, 1989.

DeRoo, Carlene and Carolyn DeRoo. *What's Right With Me: Positive Ways to Celebrate Your Strengths, Build Self-Esteem, and Reach Your Potential.* Oakland, Calif.: New Harbinger Publications, Inc., 2006.

Dictionary.com online. *http://dictionary.reference.com/browse/advocacy.* (Accessed March 30, 2007.)

Discovery Channel Website, The. *Dirty Jobs.* April 21, 2007. *http://dsc.discovery.com/fansites/dirtyjobs/about/about.html.*

Flaherty, James. *Coaching: Evoking Excellence in Others.* New York: Butterworth-Heinemann, 2005.

Garcia, Lee. "Plan B (What to do When Plan A Fails)." Poker Player online. October 2, 2006. *www.pokerplayernewspaper.com/viewarticle.php?id=1504&sort=author.* (Accessed May 30, 2007.)

Gilbert, Alorie. "High-stakes start-ups." CNET News.com. June 13, 2005. *http://news.com.com/2100-1022_3-5740885.html.* (Accessed May 15, 2007.)

Gladwell, Malcolm. *Blink.* New York: Little, Brown and Company, 2005.

Gore, Gary W. *Navigating Change: A Personal Field Guide to Personal Growth.* Memphis, Tenn.: Team Trek, 2002.

Grotenstein, Jonathan and Storm Reback. *All In: The (Almost) Entirely True Story of the World Series of Poker.* New York: Thomas Dunne Books, St. Martin's Press, 2005.

Harter, James K. and E.L. Schmidt. "Business Unit Level Relationship Between Employee Satisfaction, Employee Engagement and Business Outcomes." *Journal of Applied Psychology* 87 (2002): 268—279.

Hawkins, David R. *Power vs. Force: The Hidden Determinants of Human Behavior.* Carlsbad, Calif.: Hay House, 2002.

Katzenbach, Jon R. and Douglas K. Smith. *The Wisdom of Teams: Creating the High Performance Organization.* New York: Harper Collins Publishers, 2003.

Kouzes, James M., and Barry Z. Posner. *Leadership Practices Inventory.* New York: Pfeiffer, 2003.

———. *The Leadership Challenge.* New York. John Wiley & Sons, 2002.

Krueger, Jerry and Emily Killham. "The Innovation Equation." *Gallup Management Journal*, April 12, 2007.

Lombardo, Michael M. Robert W. Eichinger. *FYI: For Your Improvement: A Guide for Development and Coaching.* Minneapolis, Minn.: Lominger Limited, Inc., 2004.

Luthans, Fred and Bruce Avolio. Chapter 16 in *Authentic Leadership Development from Positive Organizational Scholarship.* San Francisco, Calif.: Berrett-Koehler Publishers, Inc., 2003.

Merriam-Webster Online Dictionary. *www.m-w.com/dictionary/ intuition* (Accessed March 18, 2007.)

Ohm, Kathy. "Leadership and Culture: The Close Connection." *Leadership* Sept. 1, 2006. *www.thefreelibrary.com/_/print/ PrintArticle.aspx?id=152994006.* (Accessed May 4, 2007.)

Peterson, Christopher and Nansook Park. "Character Strengths in Organizations." *Journal of Organizational Behavior* 27 (2006): 1149–1154.

————. "Positive Psychology as the Evenhanded Positive Psychologist Views It." *Psychological Inquiry* 14 (2003): 141–146.

Pickett, Joseph P., ed. The *American Heritage Dictionary of the English Langu*age. Boston, Mass.: Houghton Mifflin Company, 2000.

Pladott, Dinnah, Ph.D. "Positive Psychology and Positive Organizational Scholarship." OnTrack Website. *www.ontrackcoaching.com/articles/positivepsychology.htm.* (Accessed May 2, 2007.)

Purnell, Dan. Interview with Marcus Buckingham on *The Today Show*, April 20, 2007.

Quinn, Robert. "Moments of Greatness: Entering the Fundamental State of Leadership." *Harvard Business Review* 5 (2005): 77–83.

Ray, Paul H. and Sherry Ruth Anderson. *The Cultural Creatives: How 50 Million People are Changing the World.* New York: Three Rivers Press, 2001.

Shaw, Marvin E. *Group Dynamics: The Psychology of Small Group Behavior.* New York: McGraw Hill Inc., 1971.

"Strengths: The Next Generation—A new book builds on the concepts first popularized in the bestseller Now, Discover Your Strengths." Interview with Tom Rath, *Gallup Management Journal* March 8, 2007. *http://gmj.gallup.com/content/26755/Strengths-The-Next-Generation.aspx.* (Accessed June 27, 2007.)

Tichy, Noel M. "GE's Crotonville: A Staging Ground for Corporate Revolutions." *Academy of Management Executive* 3 (1989): 99–5106.

"Understanding James Woods." Toppoker.com *www.toppoker.org/poker-players/james-woods.html.* (Accessed May 3, 2007.)

Waitley, Denis. *The Psychology of Winning.* Berkeley, Calif.: Berkeley Press, 1986.

Whitmore, John. *Coaching for Performance.* London: Nicholas Brealey Publishing, 1992.

Index

ABOUT THE AUTHORS

Andrea Sigetich plays to her strengths through her work as a leadership coach and consultant. Her business degrees are from the University of Michigan and the University of Utah, and she is a Master Certified Coach. Prior to opening her own firm, SageCoach, Inc., in 1997, Andrea held international leadership positions with General Electric, Digital Equipment, and Novell. Her clients include such diverse firms as FedEx, Clorox, AMD, and the Kellogg Foundation. She lives with her husband in Bend, Oregon, and is crazy about hiking, kayaking, and driving her 1977 Fiat Spyder in the summertime.

Carol Leavitt, MBA, is a management consultant who works with a range of organizations—from Fortune 500 companies to small, entrepreneurial firms—in industries that include healthcare, financial services, high-tech, and more. Her work, her passion, and her strengths lie in developing leaders and teams. Through coaching, training, and unique interventions, Carol engages and strengthens the skills and capabilities of managers and employees alike, enhancing their collaboration and productivity while positively im-pacting the business' bottom line. Carol's home is the desert of St. George, Utah, where she and her family pursue hiking, boating, and sports adventures (with a little theater thrown in!).

For more information about the authors and their work, visit their Website, *www.play2yourstrengths.com*.